# Amsterdam

TIMELESS TOP 10 TRAVEL GUIDES

Amsterdam Top 10 Districts, Shopping and Dining, Museums, Activities, Historical Sights, Nightlife, Top Things to do Off the Beaten Path, and Much More!

By Tess Downey

# Foreword

There are thousand reasons why tourists go and visit Amsterdam, but it isn't just one of those "one – dimensional cities" that you hear about. There's more to Amsterdam than the canals, coffee shops, and cabarets! Amsterdam is a city filled with historic, cultural, and geographical significance. This is one of those cities that rewards tourists who starts exploring, and someone who doesn't go "by the book" when it comes to travelling, but for the purposes of you not getting "too lost" (if there's such a thing), this book will give you an idea about the best places to visit and the best things to do in this great city so that you can save time and make the trip worth it.

Amsterdam is in itself a well – organized city, so much so that you'd think it's a city built by tourists and for tourists. Exploring the city is fairly easy and very accessible. There are a plethora of things to do regardless of when you plan to visit. Of course, the best part in any travel is to not just experience what it can offer, but to also know the people behind it. You'll surely love the culture here and it'll be one of those amazing trips to remember. Welcome to the beautiful capital of Netherlands! Welcome to Amsterdam!

# Table of Contents

# Amsterdam: The Venice of the North

Amsterdam is one of Europe's best preserved cities dating back to the 17th century. The "Venice of the North" has a fun contemporary sort of edge to it, and it's also a progressive city that's invigorated by a time – honored spirit of "live and let live." Amsterdam is mostly known for its breathtaking picturesque canals, coffee shops that don't serve coffees, free – spirited commuters that go around the city using bicycles, outstanding contributions from world –

renowned artists like Rembrandt and Van Gogh, the famous diary and life story of Anne Frank as well as the edgy and quite controversial Red Light District.

The rich history of the city is very much the same and significant today as when it was laid out during the 1600s at the time of Holland's golden age. Back in the $13^{th}$ century, the city's founders built a dam on the Amstel. The people who eventually lived in this area were named after Amstel Dam which eventually became Amsterdam.

Amsterdam's city – center known as Damrak was once the main canal. Today, this area connects the train station to the city center and Main Square. From that point forward, you'll see the many wonderful sights of the city filled with various bridges and canals. During Netherland's golden age, wealthy Dutch merchants built the great city of Amsterdam upon piles of wooden chips which resulted into what we see today – a wonderland of canals that's lined up with beautifully structured town houses and trees.

Amsterdam is generally a very safe city. You don't have to worry about violent crimes against foreigners because it's very rare, but petty crimes like pickpocketing are quite common especially in various tourist spots. The best thing to do of course is to always be mindful of your pockets and belongings, and try not to catch bad people's attention with your bling.

The Venice of the North offers everything a traveller and even a local tourist want, and with a determination to embrace the wonders of life, people who wish to visit this place just like you can surely contribute to that ultimate memento of a much broader perspective.

# Chapter One: Amsterdam Overview

According to author Geert Mark, "Amsterdam is a city, but it is also a country by itself, a small nation inside a larger one." Amsterdam is not just a city that's unique from the rest of Netherlands; it's also the most exceptional city in the whole world. If you compare it to other cities, you may conclude that it's truly like no other. I know that seems to be a bold statement but I'm quite sure you'll arrive at the same conclusion when you've been here, and have travelled to a lot of places.

The main reason lies with its people and the way the whole city is built. There are 175 nationalities that resides in the city, what could be more multi – cultural than that? The city has an appeal of a mashed up century old and modern – day metropolis but at the same time it's not huge enough to be considered as a village that's filled with many wonders to discover unlike other cities. It's quite enchanting, romantic, and spontaneous. It truly has that notion of "live and let live."

*Amsterdam in Focus*

The Golden Age of Netherlands helped the city grow in various aspects especially in trade and architecture. Amsterdam is one of those picture – perfect cities that any millennial will die to snap a selfie from; one of its historic feature that's quite prominent everywhere you look is the gabled houses. Gable houses are built along the world famous bridges and canals in the city. The gable types were used to mask the architectural idiosyncrasies through the sharp and pitched roofs. The city just wouldn't be the same without such neighborhoods, it's as important as the canals that made the city what it is today.

There are around 1,200 bridges in the city that connects everything and makes every destination very accessible. It's actually included as one of the biggest must – see in Amsterdam. You can admire 15 bridges at the same time if you happen to stop between Reguliersgracht and Herengracht. Now tell me, how many cities in the world offers this kind of experience? Only in Amsterdam!

The Canal Ring which is locally known as 'Grachtengordel' as well as the 165 bridges and canals including gable houses are now part of the World Heritage Site (UNESCO).

Unlike other famous European cities, Amsterdam doesn't have any squares or palaces that's built during the ancient times, making it one of a kind. Majority of the city was built by architects from the 20th century; you won't find huge structure built during the time of the ancient or medieval era just like in most cities. As what locals say, the charm is in the detail. What you can mostly find are gable stones that date back to the Middle – Ages.

The special thing about it is that, those stones engraved the names of the house owner's details, profession, history, and other depictions and interesting discoveries making it much more interesting. You just have to really be keen and appreciate the subtle details because that's what makes Amsterdam quite unique.

The city is a cultural hotspot today with a population of more than 745,000 from over 170 nationalities. This is a clear message to the world that everyone is welcome regardless of their race, religion, and background.

### *A Brief History of Amsterdam and the Netherlands*

Before Amsterdam became known as the "Venice of the North" and before it became one of Europe's most beautifully preserved city, it had gone through different significant events throughout history; let's take a look at its colorful past so we can appreciate the city's present, and look forward to its future.

- 1150 to 1300: Dams are built to retain the IJ River that is between Haarlem and Zuiderzee. This is the place where herring fishermen lived and built a community. They settled along the banks of the Amstel River.

- 1220: A barrier known as "The Amstel Dam" was built by the city's founders (mostly by wealthy Dutch nationals) in order to control the tidal waves of Zuiderzee. This dam was built at the mouth of the Amstel River; eventually people began calling the place Amsterdam.

- 1275: The Amsterdam is founded right after the count of Holland granted a toll – free status to the residents who live along the Amstel River or the Amstel Dam. It eventually became a city, and gained its first direct access to the ocean through the Zuiderzee which is now known as Ijsselmeer.

- 1380: The Medieval Canter that can be found in modern day Amsterdam was dug in order to build several canals and bridges that connected the city. Amsterdam eventually flourished, and even went on to having full control over the sea trade in

Scandinavia. It later gained free access to the Baltic that eventually broke the Hansa monopoly.

- 1452: New building laws were made because of the fire that broke out in the city – center which burned and devoured timber frames. The decree stated that buildings, houses, and structures in the future should be made out of bricks and tiles to prevent such circumstances.

- 1519: During this time Charles V of Spain was crowned as the Holy Roman Emperor. Amsterdam became a part of the Spanish empire through various treaties, royal marriages, and dynasties. Catholicism became the main religion of the city and the whole country of Netherland. Protestant faith was also tolerated in the city.

- 1535: Anabaptists occupied Amsterdam's city hall. The motto of this group is "Truth is Naked" which is why they are naked when they made the rebellion.

They were defeated by the authorities of the city and were brutally executed after a bloody battle.

- 1566 to 1568: The Low Countries revolted against King Philip II of Spain due to lack of religious freedom and also because of King Philip's repressive act. This prompted a war that lasted for over 80 years. The rebels at the time won the first battle in a place called Friesland. This battle was eventually immortalized in the country's national anthem.

- 1578: Amsterdam fell from the so – called Watergeuzen or sea beggars which are Calvinist brigands. The city was captured in a bloodless coup around this time. And because of this, about one year later, William the Silent and the people of Netherlands eventually created a Dutch Republic consisting of 7 provinces.

- 1618: Catholicism became outlawed though clandestine worship is still tolerated. During this time, a trade – oriented newspaper known as

Courante Uyt Italien, Duyts – Landt & Co. was printed in the city; it's also known as one of the first regular newspapers in the world. At this time, Amsterdam is already a leading publisher of atlases, public maps, and sea charts.

- 1688: William III repelled the French, with the help of Spain, Prussia, and Austria. William III of Orange eventually invaded Great Britain where William was proclaimed King together with his wife, Queen Mary Stewart.

- 1795: French soldiers during this time occupied Netherlands including the Amsterdam area. The French installed a Batavian Republic which was named after the Batavi Tribe that famously rebelled against the emperor of Rome in 69 A.D. The fragmented provinces eventually became a centralized state and made Amsterdam the capital of Netherlands.

- 1813 to 1814: The French troops were overthrown and William VI of Orange was crowned as a Dutch King. He became known as William I. The Austrians eventually relinquished their claims of the Northern and Southern provinces. The north and south joined forces and became the United Kingdom of Netherlands.

- 1830: The French helped the southern provinces to become independent and form the Kingdom of Belgium. In 1839, the country was recognized by the Dutch government.

- 1865 to 1876: This was the time of rapid social and economic change. The Dutch railway system was further expanded by digging up the North Sea Canal. Socialist principles were also established in the government.

- 1914 to 1920: Netherlands was neutral during World War I. However, the country eventually experienced food shortage that led to strikes, and support for the Dutch Communist Party.

- 1940: Germany invaded Netherlands, and Rotterdam was destroyed by the Luftwaffe. Amsterdam, on the other hand, didn't suffer as much damage. During this time, a Dutch exile government was set up by Queen Wilhemina in London.

- 1944 to 1945: The Allies liberated the southern region of the Netherlands. However, the southern and northern regions were cut off from food and water supplies. Millions of Dutch died from the so – called "Hunger Winter."

- 1975: The Netherlands enacted different laws concerning illegal drugs although possession of a small amount of weed or marijuana is de – criminalized. Also, during this time, the Nieuwmarkt District is where squatters and authorities fought over the construction of the metro system.

- 1980: Queen Beatrix marries Claus von Arnsberg (a German diplomat). The occasion was disrupted by a smoke bomb and some people created a riot at the dam.

- 2001: Same – sex marriage was officially legalized in the country. Netherlands is the first ever country to legalize such law. The same – sex marriage act was eventually followed by other countries including Spain, South Africa, Belgium, and Canada a few years after it was passed in the Netherlands.

- 2002: Pim Fortuyn was assassinated. He was the country's leading politician at the time, and someone who is a hard – liner on immigration. The ruling Dutch parties suffered major losses during the national election.

- 2004: Theo van Gogh, an activist filmmaker and also a fierce critic of Islamis religion, was assassinated creating intense debates over the limits of a multicultural society.

## *Language, People and Culture*

The Dutch people have a flair or natural ability for social engineering. The people built a society that's custom made for different interest, activities, and social groups. This is why when you get there you'll see that there are various churches that'll suit different kinds of faith, separate sports clubs, unions, political parties etc.

There's a famous Dutch saying "Act normal, that's crazy enough" this is how eccentric the public can be as they go about things without any comment. As a society and as a culture, they are pretty much tolerant of anything. They are also quite irrepressibly sociable and have some a characteristic of having a moralistic streak which is something that was passed on from Calvinists, their predecessors. They are stunningly frank and blunt towards other people but it's usually coming from a desire to be honest. They are the kind of people who likes to critique but they do so with a sense of humor.

When it comes to women in the society, most of them are quite confident on a social level but some are still old – fashioned and is taken for granted, so to speak. As for gays and lesbians, they are very much accepted in the society. As what we've mentioned earlier, Amsterdam is the first ever city that allowed same – sex marriage. They also have laws against discrimination due to sexual orientation. The homosexual communities in Amsterdam enjoy freedom and they are also morally accepted by society in general. Dutch people in general are friendly though they tend to be quite blunt and direct to people but you will surely enjoy their honesty if you learn how to appreciate their cultural background.

You don't need to learn the Dutch language when you go to Amsterdam or any part of Netherlands. It's not compulsory as locals know how to speak English, though it will surely help on your trip and perhaps make you connect more with the locals. What foreigners love about learning a bit of Dutch is the opportunity to pronounce words of diphthongs which are vowel combinations in grammar. You'll get to say the throat – clearing sound of words with ch's and g's (as in Van Gogh: pronounced as Van GOKH).

Tourists who tried to speak Dutch are usually met with quizzical looks from the locals especially when they attempt to do the crazy pronunciations but it usually warms their heart when they can see the effort in doing so.

# Chapter Two: Travel Essentials

Amsterdam is a really cool and vibrant city but there are some things you need to keep in mind before taking the trip to the Venice of the North so that you won't be caught off guard, you won't get into trouble, and navigating around will be much easier for you and your family. This chapter will include all the essentials you need as a traveller including the credit cards/ debit cards you need to use when paying for transactions, the best time to go, the seasons/climate, the communication services available, and the hotlines you can call in cases of emergency. We also included a list of don'ts when visiting this gabled city so that you will stay safe and equip you with all the things you need to make this trip an awesome experience.

*Traveller's Info*

Check out in this section the important things you need to keep in mind before you travel in Amsterdam.

**Money Exchange, ATMs, and Credit Cards**

The currency in Amsterdam and the Netherlands is Euro. 1 Euro is equal to 100 cents.

You can exchange your national money at various banks and exchanged offices in Amsterdam, or you can also exchange it inside a special office located in the Central Station. It is highly recommended that you exchange your money or withdraw notes in official money exchanges so that you'll avoid getting scammed. It might also be a good idea to exchange large sums of money so that you can get the best rates.

You can withdraw money on various ATMs where major debit cards are accepted. It is spread throughout the city including the airport or other transportation hubs as well as in major tourist spots. Credit cards such as Visa, MasterCard and American Express are accepted in various hotels, restaurants, car rentals and shops just look out for the credit card sticker posted on doors. There are shops in Amsterdam that doesn't have any cashier, and you can only pay for goods by swiping your credit or debit card so make sure to always bring your card with you, and check if it has a chip on it.

Credit or debit cards may not come in handy if you're going to eat or buy something from small businesses like food stalls, so make sure to also bring cash with you including coins so that you can easily purchase stuff from vending machines.

**Electricity and Voltage**

The standard electric supply in Amsterdam and the Netherlands is 230 volt to 50Hz AC. The plugs in the city have 2 round pins. You may need a transformer or converter to aid your electrical equipment or appliances. It is highly recommended that you buy adaptors at various convenience and electrical/gadget stores in your own country so you can easily specify the equipment you need.

**Public Holidays**

Every day is the best time to head over to the city of Amsterdam but for your convenience; do take note of the following dates and events so you can plan ahead and avoid any hassle. The public holidays listed below means that institutions such as banks, government offices, museums and some businesses are closed or they're only open for a few hours.

- **New Year** (1 January)
- **Good Friday** (not a mandatory holiday; some businesses/ establishments might be open)
- **Easter Sunday**
- **Easter Monday**

- **Queen's Day (April 30)**
- **Liberation Day** (May 5; official holiday is only held every 5 years)
- **Ascension Day** (40 days after Easter in the Catholic religion)
- **Pentecost Sunday or Whitsunday** (7 weeks after Easter)
- **Christmas Day** (25 to 26 December)

**Opening Hours**

Businesses are open from 8 a.m. to 5 p.m. from Monday to Friday. Some shops are still open every Saturdays, only a few every Sunday. Public supermarkets/ grocery stores stay open until 10 in the evening. Shops usually stay longer even on a Sunday.

When it comes to establishments like museums, they are usually close on public holidays like Christmas and New Year. They are open weekdays from 10 a.m. to 5 – 6 p.m. It's best to check the schedule of your tour or confirm the opening hours of the museum/ gallery via their website or social media pages as it may have varying conditions.

**Communication Services**

- **Mobile Phones/Telephones**

The whole country of Netherlands is serviced by GSM 900/ 1800/ GPRS/ HSPDA mobile networks. If you have a European mobile, you don't have anything to worry about. However, for those who came from the U.S., Asia, Middle East, and other countries outside Europe, you may need to check your phone or devices for compatibility. The international access code in Netherlands is + 31 while the city code of Amsterdam is (0)20.

- **Wi-Fi/ Internet Services**

The Wi-Fi and internet services in Amsterdam are fast and accessible. You can use your free Wi – Fi connection at the hotel you're staying in and you can also connect for free when you dine in restaurants, local pubs, coffee shops, and cafes, you may just need to ask the waiters/ staff if it's password protected. You can also go to internet cafes but it will cost you around 2 Euros and it may be quite slow.

You can check the following internet resources to help you navigate better in the city or in the whole country by going to these links:

- **Official Tourist Website for Netherlands:** www.holland.com
- **Official Tourist Website for Amsterdam:** www.iamsterdam.com

*Best Time to Go*

As I've mentioned earlier, every time is the best time to visit this wonderful city, and that's because there's something to look forward to and enjoy at any given month. Festivals, events, concerts, and celebrations are non – stop, and even if there's not much going on, many museums and galleries hold various mini events/ exhibitions.

During summertime, the locals and tourists alike flock into the city streets, cafes, canals, and parks to simply enjoy the outdoors. Perhaps the best time to go to Amsterdam during summertime is filled with open – air festivities like concerts, theatrical performances, and the likes which are usually free! Tourists and locals also look forward to the Queen's day which is a public holiday that is held every 30th of April; it's kind of a party that ends all parties in the city, so to speak.

In addition to all of this, other major cultural events that you might enjoy happens around the month of June (Holland Fest, Roots Music Fest), July (Julidan), and August (Uitmarkt). If you love cycling, why not join in the National Cycling Day or join a road race that happens throughout the whole year.

When it comes to accommodation, the best time to go to is around November to December because this is when hotels are very cheap especially around the succeeding months of January to February, so take advantage of that.

## *Climate and Weather*

The best thing about going to the Netherlands is that it's a country that has one of the best climates in Europe. It has a maritime climate which means that it has mild summers, and quite cold but bearable winters. However, wind and rain showers are very common all year round especially in the months of July and August. March is the driest month in the city. The winds are quite strong especially along the coastal area.

### Wet Season

The rainfalls in the Netherlands are very unpredictable because you can still experience showers even during the dry periods (April to September).

### Spring and Fall

March to May and September to October are considered in the country as shoulder seasons. Flowers bloom around May, and the weather is also quite warm around this time which is why it's one of the best times to travel.

**Summer**

Summers starts from June to August. It's quite hot but not in an extreme way. Summer is the best time to do long walks in the city, and go around it via the canals. Average temperature during summer is around 64 degrees Fahrenheit.

**Winter**

Winter starts in November until February. You can experience freezing temperatures during these months. Expect a snow and fog in the whole city. The average temperature drops to as low as 2 degrees Celsius. This is why not a lot of tourists go during this period but for some people, they take advantage of the very low hotel/ accommodation rates.

*Don't's of Visiting in the Netherlands*

**Don't #1: Don't call the country Holland, call it The Netherlands**

Holland is only 2 of the 12 counties in The Netherlands. However, the reason why most tourist sometimes refer to the Netherlands as Holland is because that's where Amsterdam (and all the major tourist destinations) is located. You can make more local friends inside and outside the capital if you call it as the Netherlands.

**Don't #2: Don't think that the whole Netherlands is only Amsterdam**

This is quite common among tourists and foreigners who obviously didn't research the country that they're going into. The canals, gable houses, beautiful bridges, windmills, and various spots like museums etc. can also be found in the other regions of the country that are also worth exploring.

**Don't #3: Don't be stupid when it comes to alcohol and drug consumption**

First time visitors to Amsterdam includes them going to the notorious Red Light District, and there's nothing wrong with that. It's one of the highlights about the city but sometimes, some people go out of hand especially when it comes to handling certain things like alcohol and (illegal/ recreational) drugs. The Dutch people don't mind you getting stoned or drunk but make sure that if you plan on doing that with your friends or colleagues, you ought to be responsible about it so that you won't get into trouble with the locals and also with the other tourists around. Never do drugs in the street or buy from people in the street, if you really want to try and do it, go to the coffee shop or someplace "safe."

**Don't #4: Don't just bite into any street/fried food in Amsterdam because it's extremely hot!**

The Dutch people like their food hot, not just hot – extremely hot! If you roam around the streets of Amsterdam, there's tons of street food and tiny treats to choose from, and while it's very delicious and tasty, some tourists aren't aware that the locals like to be served with something hot, making the foreigners burn their tongues off. This includes the sauce by the way, so be very careful especially if you're visiting with your kids.

**Don't #5: Don't Wander into the Bicycle Lanes**

Never walk, stop, or wander around in the bike zone, unless you want to get hit! Trust me; you don't want to suffer from any injury or get into trouble while you're having a trip in this gorgeous city. The Dutch and the tourists will, of course still try not to hit you but as long as you're in the bike zone, they can "legally hit" you if you know what I mean. So better get out of their way, most especially if you are walking with your little kids or an elderly because it doesn't matter, they will continue riding otherwise they might also get hit with other riders coming by. If you're the one renting the bike, make sure to not ride it in the pedestrian zone, otherwise you'll be penalized for that so make sure you get off your bike and walk it if you're passing the pedestrian lane.

**Don't #6: Don't take the Dutch attitude personally or don't get offended**

As I've said earlier in the culture section of this book, Dutch people are very direct and sometimes or should I say, most times, they are really brutally honest. It doesn't matter whether you're in the Red Light District or fancy coffee shops or you're out in the street just walking, the locals may make comments about you, or directly ask you a question that usually can offend anybody. An example is, let's say your fat. Dutch people may come and tell you, "hey, why are you fat?" or "Why is your bike chain worth more than your bike?" They're intention is to not really insult you (although that's given), but they just want to know why your fat or why your bike is cheaper than the chain. They're curious but they are stunningly blunt in expressing their feelings or queries towards people.

Tourists, especially in the service industry, usually get offended by this kind of attitude. An example is that, whenever you're in a restaurant, it will usually take quite some time before the waiter come to your table even if they already saw you come in. Another tip is to also not forget to ask for your bill when you go out; they're not going to come to you sometimes like how it usually is when you're in a restaurant. That's just really how Dutch people are, being brutally honest is part of their culture, and perhaps what really makes them unique as a society.

**Don't #7: Don't ever forget to bring your credit card/ debit card**

Make sure that you always bring with you your credit card (that contains a chip and a pin number because other cards don't and it may not be acceptable). There are many shops and stores in Amsterdam that doesn't have any cashier, and the only way to pay for your stuff is through a self – serving cashier booth that only accepts credit/debit cards with a chip on it. You can easily make your transaction if you have your card with you.

**Don't #8: Don't forget to bring some Dutch coins with you**

There are also tons of vending machines that serve hot foods and sandwiches but it doesn't accept cards, only coins. If you want to save up a bit on your expenses, it's wise to also bring coins with you. There are money exchange booths around but in some places, that's not always the case so it's better if you have your coins ready.

**Don't #9: Don't be surprised if you see Dutch tourism stereotyping**

Expect to see lots of bridges, canals, coffee shops, houses made out of gable stones, bikes, cheese, tall Dutch people etc. and don't be too surprise about it to the point that you come across as someone ignorant. Be prepared for all the 'weird' things you'll see in the city, and of course you can admire it but don't overdo it, if you know what I mean as it will come as if you're stereotyping them.

**Don't #10: Don't forget to swipe your train ticket when you get on and off the train**

You need to ensure that you buzz your ticket in whenever you're going to ride the train because that's how they'll check passengers. Even if the gate is already open, still swipe your card in in the train stations. When you're getting out, make sure to also swipe your card because there's no return ticket or stuff like that. Trains in Amsterdam are very efficient, clean, and fast. It'll be a breeze when you're touring the city via trains. It'll only take about 30 minutes to get from different places, 1 -2 hours tops if the place is really far so make sure to be mindful of your belongings and don't forget to check in and out of the station using your train ticket/card.

**Don't #11: Don't take photos of girls in the windows of the Red Light District in Amsterdam**

This is just the rule when you go to this quite popular district. If they saw you, your phone might get thrown off the canal or whatever, so just try to respect this rule so that you won't get into trouble.

**Don't #12: Don't do the hop on/ hop off bus in the city**

This is because the buses can't go to a lot of places unlike in other cities since there are canals and bridges everywhere. The bus only goes around the periphery of the city and it might not be worth it. If you want to go around, it's best that you ride a boat via the canals or just rent a bike.

**Don't #13: Don't forget to bring a jacket!**

This is a must! It doesn't matter if it's summer or not, it's quite cold in Amsterdam and all of the Netherlands. This will also serve as your protection from unexpected rain showers because even if the sun is shining there are isolated rain showers throughout the day. Be prepared so that you won't get sick or be drenched in while you're touring around the country.

# Chapter Three: Getting In and Around Amsterdam

Roaming around one of Europe's busiest cities, Amsterdam boasts excellent transportation systems that will enable any foreign traveller to easily explore its hidden gems. You can do so via air links, efficient train and metro systems, and through their bicycle lanes. Once you get here, you'll realize that the city is only a walk away from everything you need to experience and see. You can traverse the city center within 30 minutes, and reach the outskirts in just 1 to 2 hours. The tram system in the city is efficient and reliable but locals prefer roaming around using their bikes – this is perhaps the best way for you to really soak in the culture and the sights, and see the city from a local's perspective.

This chapter will provide you with information as to how you can get in and around the city of Amsterdam. However, do keep in mind that the information given here is particularly subject to change. The details that'll be given here should only be used as a guide to give you an idea on the ways you can navigate the city but it's not a substitute for your own updated research.

### *Transport via Air*

The Schiphol Airport is the main international airport in the Netherlands, and it's only about 18 kilometers away from Amsterdam's city – center. It's also the 4$^{th}$ busiest airport terminal in all of Europe. You can find over 100 direct flights and airline connections to various continents around the world coming in and out of this airport.

In addition to that, the Schiphol Airport is also the hub of various international brands and shopping centers. Once you landed here, you'll end up in the arrival area known as the Schiphol Plaza. Luggage can be deposited at the Left Luggage Office, and lockers are also available. For airport and flight details, you can check out their official website at www.schiphol.nl

### *Getting into Town from the Airport*

From the Schiphol Plaza, you can take the Nederlandse Spoorwegen railway to take you to the Central Station. Trains come every 10 to 15 minutes. Make sure to buy your train ticket before going down to the escalator from the plaza's central court.

You can also choose to hail a taxi from the Schiphol Airport to central Amsterdam. It'll take around 45 minute tops, and will cost you around 30 to 40 Euros. You can contact the Amsterdam Airport Business Taxi if you want to arrive at the city in style as they offer luxury cars with professional drivers.

If you're hotel reservation includes a free shuttle service from the airport, better ask them where you can hop on. There are also public services buses like the Conexxion Interliner 370 travels to and from the city; this bus shuttle service will cost around 12.50 Euros for a one way trip, and around 19.50 Euros for a return trip. Once you make your hotel reservations, ask them if the shuttle stops on the hotel's route.

If you want to get into the city via a rental car, you can take the A4 Freeway to and from the A10 ring road around the city. Car – rental shops are found near the central exits of the airport.

## *Getting Around Amsterdam via Bicycle and Motorcycle*

Majority of the locals get around the city using fietsen (Dutch for bikes). There are around 600,000 bicycles around town every day including motorcycles. Tourists usually rent a bike to traverse the city easily. As mentioned in the previous chapter, you can ride the bike in the designated bike lanes. Never ride it while you're crossing a pedestrian street (you have to walk it) otherwise you'll be fined. If you wish to bring the bike aboard a train, you need to purchase a bike ticket or pass which can cost around €6. It's valid throughout the whole Netherlands, and you can also rent a bike around the train stations. Tourists who wish to go to other regions of Netherlands can also rent/buy a collapsible bike inside the train and carry it for free.

### *Renting a Bike or Scooter*

The rental companies listed below requires a cash deposit or a credit card imprint plus a valid ID and passport (if you're a foreigner). The bike rental includes gears, handbrakes, and coaster – brake type of bikes. You may need to pay an additional amount if you wish to have insurance.

**Bike City**

**Tel:** 626 37 21

**Website:** www.bikecity.nl

**Price Range:** €8.50/ €41 per day/week plus credit card imprint deposit

**Damstraat Rent – a – Bike**

**Tel:** 625 50 29

**Website:** www.bikes.nl

**Price Range:** € 7/ €31 per day/week plus credit card imprint deposit

**Holland Rent – a – Bike**

**Tel:** 622 32 07

**Price Range:** €6.40/ €34.50 per day/week plus €150 and credit card imprint deposit

**For Scooter Hire**

**Moped Rental Service Gilex**

**Tel:** 623 45 50

**Website:** www.gilex.nl

**Price Range:** weekday/weekend day €37.50/42.50, weekend/week €80/210 plus deposit of €450

**Some Bicycle Rules:**

- Cyclists should ride their bikes in the designated bicycle lanes.
- Watch out for pedestrians as some unfamiliar tourists wander around the bike lanes.
- It's required by law to use the front and rear bike lights after dusk. There should also be reflectors on both the wheels.
- Give a quick ring of a bell as your horn if there are people passing by your way. If you're about to hit someone or vice – versa, it's best to give a sharp yell.
- Chain your bike if you're going to leave it on the street unattended. The bikes in Amsterdam usually come with 2 locks (front/ rear).

### *Getting Around via Canal Boats, Canal Bus, Canal Bikes and Ferries*

If you truly want to see the beauty of Amsterdam, you can do so via riding the canal boats. The Canal Bus Company goes to different routes in between the Rijksmuseum and the Central Station from 9:50 am to 8 pm. If you purchase a day pass (€18 for adults; €12 for children), it's valid until noon time of the next day. You can also rent a canal bike or pedal boats; it'll cost you around €8 per pax per hour. The docks for canal boats and bikes are near the Anne Frank Museum.

If you want to ride a ferry, you can do so for free! Dock is located behind the Central Station. It usually takes passengers to the Amsterdam Noord. It may cost you just €1 if the ferry goes to the Eastern Docklands.

### *Getting Around via Car*

We do not recommend you renting a car to roam around the city, if you're not planning to travel to other far - off towns in the country but if you must, then read on.

Foreign tourists are entitled to drive in the Netherlands using their foreign license for only 185 days per year. If you're going to stay longer, you must apply for a Dutch license. You can contact the National Transport Authority at 0900 – 07 – 39.

The minimum driving age is 18 years old for cars, and 16 years for motorcycles. Traffic in the city is usually on the right side and it's generally a busy road. Seat belts are of course required, and children below 12 years old should be in the back of the vehicle.

- When driving, always be alert for bicycle riders especially if you're turning right, bikes have priority in Amsterdam.
- Trams also have the right of way so take note of that.

- The blood – alcohol limit in the city when driving is 0.05%.
- The speed limits are at 50 km per hour in built – up areas, and 80 km per hour in the whole country; 100 km per hour on major rural roads, and 100 to 120 km per hour on freeways.

**Renting a Car**

Local car rental businesses offer a much cheaper rate compared to big companies. The rates for local car companies usually start at €34 per day for 2 person cars, and €40 per day for a 4 person car. However, the rates constantly change so make sure to inquire about it first. If you're going to rent a car near the Schiphol Airport, they usually have a €40 surcharge. Below is the list of known car – rental businesses in Amsterdam:

**Avis Autoverhuur**

Tel: 683 60 61

Website: www.avis.nl

**easyCar**

Website: www.easycar.nl

**Europcar**

Tel: 683 21 23

Website: www.europcar.nl

**Hertz**

Tel: 612 24 41

Website: www.hertz.nl

**National Car Rental**

Tel: 616 24 66

Website: www.nationalcar-rental.com

**Parking Information**

Parking your car in Amsterdam is quite expensive. The so – called Pay and Display usually applies in the central area from 9 a.m. until midnight from Monday to Saturday, and noon time to midnight every Sunday. It will cost you around €4.60/27.60/18.40 per hour/day/evening in central Amsterdam, and €3.60/21.60/14.40 outside the city – center or within the Canal belt. Prices for parking lowers as you move away from the city – center. You will be fined with an amount of around €103 at the time of this writing if you don't pay for parking.

*Getting Around via Taxi*

We also do not recommend you getting around the city or outside the city – center using a taxi because Amsterdam taxis are one of the most expensive rides in Europe. The worst thing about it is that the drivers aren't familiar with the streets so you need to tell them how to get to your destination, at least now; you have Waze apps and Google maps to help you out.

If you need to really ride a cab, you can hail them at stop zones and at taxi stands which is usually around hotel lobbies. The flat rate is €3.40 and €1.94 per kilometer plus a 5 to 10% tip for the driver.

### *Getting around via Train*

Trains serve the public at regular intervals (every 5 to 6 times per hour) for domestic destinations. The main train station in the city is called the Centraal Station (CS/ Central Station). The trains are safe, clean, and efficient; this is perhaps the easiest and cost – effective way to get around Amsterdam and also reach the outskirts of town.

Tickets for domestic destinations can be purchased at the window or via the ticketing machines. If you're going to buy the ticket on board, you'll double the normal fare so make sure to buy the ticket before hopping on the train.

If you are planning to do lot of travelling, then it's best that you purchase a one – day travel ticket which can cost you around €40 at the time of this writing.

# Chapter Four: Hotels and Accommodations

The city of Amsterdam boasts many charming hotels and wonderful accommodations. Most of the hotels or spaces you'll get to see around the city have great locations overlooking the scenic canals and beautiful bridges as well as courtyards. Some of the hotels were once old buildings, canal houses, and industrial establishments that were transformed to beautiful lodgings – thanks to the Dutch architects who reinvented them. Some of the hotels' interiors are inspired by many artistic and historical artifacts as well as modern – day designs. However, these charming and scenic lodgings don't come cheap. If you're on a budget, your best bet is to visit the city when accommodation prices are low which is around November to January. This chapter will provide you with information on the best districts and areas to stay in while you're in Amsterdam. We also provided you with three of the best hotels around each area as well as their unique amenities.

## *1. CITY CENTER DISTRICT*

The city – center is a myriad contrast of Amsterdam's old center. If you're ready to splurge in terms of accommodation, then this is the area to do so. The reason why hotels and accommodations here aren't cheap is because it's in close proximity to almost everything Amsterdam has to offer; this is where you can find the city's medieval center, the famous Red Light District, and the gorgeous river view overlooking the canals and bridges. The guests staying in this side of town are usually reserve for the rich and famous. Here are the top 3 best hotels in the city – center:

**Medieval Center**

**Hotel De L'Europe**

**Tel: 531 17 77**

**Website: www.leurope.nl**

**Description/ Amenities/ Features:**

- Has an elegant Victorian period décor
- Has 100 huge rooms made out of marble tiles and bathrooms
- Has an Excelsior restaurant
- Has a very impressive chichi gym (recommended by former California Governor and Hollywood Star, Arnold Schwarzenegger
- Has canal boat cruise service

## Red Light District

**Nh Grand Hotel Krasnapolsky**

**Tel: 554 91 11**

**Website: www.nh-hotels.com**

**Description/ Amenities/ Features:**

- One of Amsterdam's grand hotels since 1866
- Has 468 elegant and compact rooms
- Has glorious public spaces
- Has a 19th century winter garden dining room
- Has fitness and business centers

**Nieuwmarkt**

**Misc Eat Drink Sleep**

**Tel: 330 62 41**

**Website: www.hotelmisc.com**

**Description/ Amenities/ Features:**

- Walking distance from the famous Nieuwmarkt Square
- Has only a total of six rooms with various visually – stunning room décor such as the "baroque room," "Africa room," "Room of Wonders"
- Breakfast is included in the accommodation rate, making it budget friendly place
- Has a special and equally charming room with a canal view or a garden view.
- Quite affordable for travellers who are on a budget

## 2. *JORDAAN DISTRICT*

Jordan is one of Amsterdam's most colorful district in spite of its narrow lanes and few accommodation options. You'll definitely enjoy various quirky shops nearby as well as cozy cafes. It has a very charming and unique vibe that anyone will surely enjoy, and it's also accessible to the many sights of the city. Here are the top 3 best hotels in the Jordan:

**Hotel Amsterdam Wiechmann**

**Tel: 626 33 21**

**Website: www.hotelwiechmann.nl**

**Description/ Amenities/ Features:**

- Has a beautiful canal – side location
- It's a family – run hotel
- Occupies a total of 3 houses with furnished rooms that has an antique décor.
- Quite affordable for travellers who are on a budget

**<u>International Budget Hostel</u>**

**Tel: 624 27 84**

**Website: www.internationalbudgethostel.com**

**Description/ Amenities/ Features:**

- Has a beautiful canal – side location
- A former warehouse
- Perfect for those who are into the nightlife
- Rooms has a 4 person limit
- Cool hub of backpackers from different countries

- Very cheap especially during off – season; breakfast isn't included.
- Very affordable for travellers who are on a budget.

**Christian Youth Hostel: 'The Shelter Jordan'**

**Tel: 624 47 17**

**Website: www.shelter.nl**

**Description/ Amenities/ Features:**

- It's a small and cozy hostel that's located in a quiet block, and walking distance to the tram line.
- Smoking, drinking, and spliffing is prohibited
- Has a curfew
- Rooms are clean with cheap meals throughout the day, and breakfast is also included.
- Has a garden patio where guests can relax
- Very affordable for travellers who are on a budget.

## 3. *WESTERN CANAL BELT DISTRICT*

If you're the type of person who want to stay in a district that has a century – old vibe, along with tree – lined canals and glorious mansions then the Western Canal Belt is for you. You'll see many structures such as monuments and facades. It's also in close proximity with the Jordan district, and its streets are filled with various boutique shops. Here are the top 3 best hotels in the Western Canal Belt:

**Dylan**

**Tel: 530 20 10**

**Website: www.dylanamsterdam.com**

**Description/ Amenities/ Features:**

- The designer of this gorgeous and very stylish hotel is a London native by the name of Anouska Hempel.
- Has 41 sophisticated and decorated rooms inspired by Japanese and Indonesian designs.
- Near the 17$^{th}$ century canal houses
- Rooms are filled with silk pillows, and has spacious bathrooms
- Comes with a health – club access for free

**Hotel Pulitzer**

**Tel: 523 52 35**

**Website: www.luxurycollection.com**

**Description/ Amenities/ Features:**

- The hotel is spread over 25 canal houses. It's a hotel that has a boutique – hotel charm to it.
- It has various restored rooms from one house to another.
- Has a cozy bathroom that comes with lots of extra stuff.

**Canal House Hotel**

**Tel: 622 51 82**

**Website: www.canalhouse.nl**

**Description/ Amenities/ Features:**

- Has a total of 26 beautifully designed and ornately furnished rooms
- Has a $17^{th}$ century dining room with glorious looking chandeliers, grand piano, and a view of the garden

- Has a burgundy – hued bar
- The rooms are small but have an antique décor that's very inviting to any guest.

## 4. *SOUTHERN CANAL BELT DISTRICT*

The Southern Canal Belt district is known as the cradle of Amsterdam's Golden Age. It's very near Utrechtsestraat, which is the dining hub of tourists and locals, as well as the renowned antique shop of Nieuwe Spiegelstraat. It is home to the city's swankiest hotels that can accommodate any type of traveller. Here are the top 3 best hotels in the Southern Canal Belt:

**Seven One Seven**

**Tel: 427 07 17**

**Website: www.717hotel.nl**

**Description/ Amenities/ Features:**

- One of the best hotels in the city
- It's beautifully designed and it's also quite breathtaking.
- Its 8 rooms has a plush and vibrant ambience
- Accommodation rate Comes with a breakfast, and afternoon tea

**Amsterdam American Hotel**

**Tel: 556 30 00**

**Website: www.amsterdamamerican.com**

**Description/ Amenities/ Features:**

- Filled with many contemporary furnishings
- The building is beautifully restored to its original splendor
- Has 175 rooms that are now smoke – free
- Guests also have access to the gym and sauna
- This is also where Café Americain is located.

**Banks Mansion**

**Tel: 420 00 55**

**Website: www.banksmansion.nl**

**Description/ Amenities/ Features:**

- Has thoroughly renovated rooms and lobby area
- Has a contemporary decoration

- One of the favorite hubs of tourists who are looking for a budget – friendly accommodation.

## *5. OLD SOUTH DISTRICT*

Old South district is filled with 19th century boulevards, wide streets coupled grand museums. This place shouldn't be overlooked by hotel seekers because it's next to the renowned Concertgebouw, and some of the hotels houses art works of Van Gogh and Rembrandt. It's also in close proximity to the city – center. Here are the top 3 best hotels in the Old South:

**<u>Hilton Amsterdam</u>**

**Tel: 710 60 00**

**Website: www.hilton.com**

**Description/ Amenities/ Features:**

- It's quite an old – school hotel that's usually for business guests
- Has quite a history since this is the hotel where Beatle's band member John Lennon and Yoko Ono staged their world peace performance in 1969.
- Rooms have an international business standard
- Has a grassy park with marina
- Has a sauna, Turkish bath, and health club amenties

**Xaviera Hollander Bed & Breakfast**

**Tel: 673 39 34**

**Website: www.xavierahollander.com**

**Description/ Amenities/ Features:**

- The interior decoration has many racy allusions of Xaviera from her past life. Xaviera is a former star from a show called Happy Hooker, and was once a center of media – attention.
- The rooms are uniformly luxurious
- Some rooms also comes with a garden hut
- Quite affordable for travellers who are on a budget.

**Collector**

**Tel: 673 67 79**

**Website: www.the-collector.nl**

**Description/ Amenities/ Features:**

- It's a contemporary renovation of a 1914 building
- The style of the rooms and the overall space is furnished with museum – style displays such as wooden shoes, Amsterdam school furnishings, and old clocks.
- Each room has its own balcony
- The best part is that the owner can buy food for you to prepare for breakfast at your leisure

## 6. *VONDELPARK AREA*

The Vondelpark area has a wealthy vibe to it. It's a place filled with history, and it's a privileged urban life. One of the most admired characteristic of the neighborhood around Vondelpark is that it is free of class pretension. You'll see what I mean once you saw employees from banks and government agencies casually exercise and jog around the park. Here are the top 3 best hotels around Vondelpark:

**Fusion Suites**

**Tel: 618 46 42**

**Website: www.fusionsuites.com**

**Description/ Amenities/ Features:**

- It's just a few distance away from the hustle and bustle of another famous tourist spot which is the Museumplein
- The suits are quite spacious, and the location is nestled in a quiet neighborhood.
- Tourists and locals alike describe it as a comfortable lodging without being over the top.
- Its rooms are complete with TVs, computers, cocomat poster beds, and a tasteful interior décor of Eastern earth tones.
- Accommodation comes with tasty treats and breakfast.
- Quite affordable for travellers who are on a budget.

**Hotel Roemer**

**Tel: 589 08 00**

**Website: www.vondelhotels.com**

**Description/ Amenities/ Features:**

- A cozy and gorgeous hotel
- Located in a calm and serene location that's walking distance to Vondelpark and the Museum Quarter
- All the rooms overlook a garden or a leafy street
- Quite affordable for travellers who are on a budget.
- Rooms are filled with natural light
- Business guests will love the ergonomic workspace that it offers as well as the room service.
- Breakfast can be quite expensive.

**Hotel Vondel**

**Tel: 612 01 20**

**Website: www.vondelhotels.com**

**Description/ Amenities/ Features:**

- A chic hotel that's spread over newly renovated 7 houses to accommodate guests
- The rooms have been upgraded with a minimalist sort of style yet still has a beautiful décor
- Offers hotel discounts especially during the off – season.
- Very affordable for travellers who are on a budget.

## *7. DE PIJP DISTRICT*

The De Pijp district is right next to the Southern Canal Belt district that's located in a quiet place. It has a certain ethnic vibe to it because of the neighborhoods around the area. The district is also filled with newly renovated hotels and lodgings as well as fantastic restaurants. Here are the top 3 best hotels in De Pijp:

**Hotel Aalborg**

**Tel: 676 03 10**

**Website: www.aalborg.nl**

**Description/ Amenities/ Features:**

- The rooms are neat, clean, and newly installed.
- The front rooms has a great view of the lush Sarphatipark
- It's very accessible to the city – center; it only takes about 10 minutes to central Amsterdam which is why the area around is the hub of tourists and weekend breakers who are on a budget as rates becomes cheap during the week.
- Perfect for tourists who are on a budget

**Between Art & Kitsch B&B**

**Tel: 679 04 85**

**Website: www.between-art-and-kitsch.com**

**Description/ Amenities/ Features:**

- The rooms are beautifully decorated with various arts.

- You can see a crystal chandelier inside the baroque room
- Has artistically designed tile work
- Has great view of the Rijksmuseum
- It's a 3 – story building that's situated in the quiet canal area at the edge of De Pijp.
- Rooms are non – smoking
- Lovely hosts, and budget friendly for travellers

**Bicycle Hotel Amsterdam**

**Tel: 679 34 52**

**Website: www.bicyclehotel.com**

**Description/ Amenities/ Features:**

- If you're the type of tourist who is into a "bed and bike thing," then this is the lodge for you.
- The hotel has a casual and friendly ambience
- Rooms are very comfortable and accommodation comes with an organic breakfast!

- You can also rent carrier bikes that are great for city tours with your kids.

## 8. *PLANTAGE, EASTERN ISLANDS & EASTERN DOCKLANDS*

If you're kind of used to thinking outside the box, then this district/s is for you. The hotels and accommodations in the eastern suburbs of Amsterdam offer quite a charming vibe that can never be found in the old center. The buildings are filled with lushes trees, cutting – edge architecture, and a great scenic view of riverboats. Tourists usually come home here after a great party downtown. Here are the top 3 best hotels in Plantage and Dockland area:

**Plantage Area**

**<u>Eden Lancaster Hotel</u>**

**Tel: 535 68 88**

**Website: www.edenhotelgroup.com**

**Description/ Amenities/ Features:**

- It has a total of 93 spacious rooms, and the building is next to a park
- Recently underwent a top to toe renovation
- It's regarded by tourists and locals as one of the smartest accommodations in the Plantage district.
- Rooms are complete with amenities such as TV, phone, Wi – Fi, bathroom etc.

- It has great room décor such as blonde wood, cream, red brick, and a stylized St. Andrew's cross of the city seal.
- Breakfast is not included but it's very affordable.

**Eastern Docklands Area**

**<u>Mövenpick Hotel City Centre</u>**

**Tel: 519 12 00**

**Website: www.moevenpick-hotels.com**

**Description/ Amenities/ Features:**

- Located in the water's edge and it's also next to the Passenger Terminal building
- It's a 20 – storey building suitable for business guests
- The building is layered with stripes of glass, white concrete, and green granite making it appealing on the outside

- Rooms have views of the harbor overlooking the cruise ships and ferries
- Walking distance to the Central Station

**Hotel Rembrandt**

**Tel: 627 27 14**

**Website: www.hotelrembrandt.nl**

**Description/ Amenities/ Features:**

- Rooms are spotless, and comes with all the important amenities like TVs, phones, and even coffeemakers
- The breakfast room is very beautiful and classy.
- It's also decorated with chandeliers and 17th century artworks

*9. Oosterpark Area*

Oosterpark is just a tram or bus ride away from central Amsterdam. The lodgings are very comfortable, spacious and also located in a quiet area but some are not of quality. Don't forget to visit the exotic Tropenmuseum while you're staying at Oosterpark area. Here's the only hotel that tourists love in this place:

**Hotel Arena**

**Tel: 850 24 00**

**Website: www.hotelarena.nl**

**Description/ Amenities/ Features:**

- Hotel Arena has morphed from a chapel to an orphanage before becoming a backpacker's hostel and renovating it to a modern day 121 room hotel.
- It has a nightclub, café, and also a trendy restaurant
- Its rooms are of minimalist design, quite spacious, and also chic.
- Breakfast isn't included but it's very affordable

## *10.OUTER DISTRICTS*

If you're planning to stay in hotels that are quite far from the hustle and bustle of the city – center, then why not consider checking in Amsterdam's outer districts? It's filled with affordable and newly renovated suits that's also complete with amenities, and has its own charming way of attracting foreign guests. Here are the top 3 best hotels in the Outer District:

**Captain's Place**

**Tel: 419 81 19**

**Website: www.meesvof.nl**

**Description/ Amenities/ Features:**

- This charming lodge is the former ore harbor of Eastern Docklands
- Rooms are quite large, neat, and has its own heated bathrooms
- Guests enjoy the on – board garden where you can take your breakfast, and relax after meal. It also has a sliding glass roof so that guests can still enjoy even during a bad weather

**Hotel V Map**

**Tel: 662 32 33**

**Website: www.hotelv.nl**

**Description/ Amenities/ Features:**

- Hotel V Map is a small hotel with quite a number of minimalist style and groovy fireplace
- It has a fresh vibe and the interior is covered with vibrant colors
- It only has 24 rooms but it's very comfortable and also complete with basic amenities
- It's in close proximity to the bars located in De Pijp district.

**Windketel**

**Tel: 682 26 66**

**Website: www.windketel.nl**

**Description/ Amenities/ Features:**

- Windketel hotel was once a part of the municipal water works.
- It's a great place for romantic getaways

- The building is quite small but very cozy, and it's also filled with state of the art appliances, wood fittings, and even a skylit bedroom!

# Chapter Five: Dining in Amsterdam

Johannes van Dam, a popular Dutch restaurant critic, once said that the Dutch would eat anything if it's well – presented, to quote "if it [the food] had a bow on it." However, Dutch cuisine is not as bad as you might think after reading this critic's comment; after all he's a critic. Dutch cuisine is a major delight for many locals and tourists alike, it's got many delicacies inspired from former colonies, and the scenic river and canals adds to the flair and flavor of the meal.

You can find lots of dining clubs, designer café houses, and international restaurant that offer various kinds of cuisine with Dutch food being the specialty. It all boils down to the way the Dutch people cook, and while it's not exactly refined, they still offer a scrumptious and honest dish like their famous hotchpotch.

When it comes to prices, eating out in Amsterdam seems reasonable compared to other European cities such as Paris, and London. Lunch meals with main courses will cost you about €8 to €18 at the time of this writing. High – end restaurants can cost you anywhere between €25 and €35 for a 3 course – meal. Breakfast, coffee drinks, and wines are quite expensive; coffee and house wines start at €5 and up at the time of this writing. Before you enter a restaurant make sure that you have cash as well because some of them don't accept credit cards. Do check it in advance. This chapter will focus on the highly recommended restaurants/ cafes in each district of Amsterdam get ready for one mouth – watering trip!

## 1. *MEDIEVAL CENTRE*

Here are the top restaurants in central Amsterdam that you can feast on:

**Supper Club**

**Tel: 638 05 13**

**Website: www.supperclub.nl**

**Description:**

- Regarded as one of the most 'lit' restaurants in the city - center
- The restaurant is an all – white, and theatrical room filled with large mattresses.
- You can dance to the beat of the DJ inside while watching quite provocative and very entertaining shows especially during their "lamb night."

**D'vijff Vlieghen**

**Tel: 530 40 60**

**Website: www.thefiveflies.com**

**Description:**

- One of the most favorite hubs of backpackers, family tourists, and business guests/
- The restaurant is spread out over $17^{th}$ century canal houses that have old – wood dining rooms bursting with colorful interior décor and interesting artifacts

- You can also find chairs where famous celebrities sat in.

**Lucius**

**Tel: 624 18 31**

**Website: www.lucius.nl**

**Description:**

- This restaurant is known for its simple yet delicious meals.
- It's always packed with tourists because it's known in offering fresh ingredients as well as various Dutch sauce and spices.
- The interior is filled with fish tank tile designs, and the ambience is fantastic.

2. *RED LIGHT DISTRICT*

Here are the top restaurants in the famed Red Light District that you can feast on:

**Blauw Aan De Wal**

**Tel: 330 22 57**

**Description:**

- It's described by Dutch critics as "rose among thorns" because it's located in the middle of the Red Light District along graffiti – covered hallways.

- It's originally a 17th century warehouse that's been renovated but the owners still kept some of the equipment around like century – old steel weights, adding to its charm.
- It also offers French and Italian cuisine
- Best to dine out in the romantic garden during the summer

<u>**Nam Kee**</u>

**Tel: 624 34 70**

**Website: www.namkee.net**

**Description:**

- If you like the taste of Asia after a few days of indulging the Dutch or European cuisines, then Nam Kee is the place to go.
- It's the most popular Chinese restaurant in this district
- Serves delicious Asian cuisine but service is quite snappy and the interior is not that attractive

**New King**

**Tel: 625 21 80**

**Website: www.newking.nl**

**Description:**

- New King is one of the fanciest and newest restaurants in the Red Light District.

- They offer one of the best roasted ducks and also comes with a full service on various meal courses.

## 3. *JORDAAN DISTRICT*

The restaurants in the Jordaan District strongly show a sociable and friendly atmosphere which has long been what this district is known for when it comes to dining out. The restaurants in the Haarlemmerstraat area are quite trendy though many tourists still eat along the Westerstraat area. If you want to check out a new dining spot, you may want to lose your way in the narrow backstreets of the district. Here are the top restaurants in Jordaan that you can feast on:

**Bordewijk**

**Tel: 624 38 99**

**Website: www.bordewijk.nl**

**Description:**

- Surprisingly, critics dub this restaurant as the "King of the Hill" even if it doesn't have a grand reputation.
- The interior is of a minimalist style and there's not much to appreciate except for their superb French and Italian cuisine.
- The chefs here are very imaginative, exceptional, and not afraid to serve something new.

**Balthazar's Keuken**

**Tel: 420 21 14**

**Website: www.balthazarskeuken.nl**

**Description:**

- Balthazar's Keuken is consistently one of the city's most top – rated restaurant but don't expect a wide –

range menu as the restaurant only offers whatever they want to offer for that day

- The interior has a modern – day rustic appeal to it with very friendly staff
- Reservations are highly recommended.

## 4. *WESTERN CANAL BELT*

The Western Canal Belt district may not have the dining diversity compared to other towns in Amsterdam but it absolutely makes up for it with some of the most interesting cafes and local restaurants that match the boutiques around.

Here are the top restaurants in the Western Canal Belt district that you can feast on:

<u>**Christophe**</u>

**Tel: 625 08 07**

**Website: www.christophe.nl**

**Description:**

- This restaurant offers lobster dishes and duck – liver terrine as part of their specialties.
- It's a Jean-Christophe Royer's Michelin-starred restaurant that's bustling with hungry guests every single night.
- They also serve herring fish here since the locals love to eat raw fish.
- It's one of the most extraordinary restaurants not just in the city but in world standards.

**De Belhamel**

**Tel: 622 10 95**

**Website: www.debelhamel.nl**

**Description:**

- In a warm weather, you can thoroughly enjoy their canal – side tables while being surrounded by fantastic Art Nouveau interior
- They serve the one of the best French and Italian cuisine in the district, and their silky roast beef is to die for.

## 5. *SOUTHERN CANAL BELT DISTRICT*

The Southern Canal Belt offers both the good and the bad, so to speak. We don't recommend you dining out in Leidseplein and Rembrandtplein area even if it's cheap and has a cheerful vibe to it because some of the restaurants aren't particularly distinctive. However, if you are staying in this area and want to find the best options, you can simply head to Utrechtsestraat where you can find the district's finest. Here are the top restaurants in the Southern Canal Belt district that you can feast on:

**Van Vlaanderen**

**Tel: 622 82 92**

**Description:**

- We highly recommend this French restaurant because aside from the scenic canal views, you'll have one of the best dining experience because the owner itself will chat with you! Owner, Bas Verstift will advise you on what wine goes with what dish and the likes.
- Their specialties include tuna carpacaccio with avocado, and chicken with bacon mousse or langoustines among others.
- Has great ambience and friendly staff

**La Rive**

**Tel: 622 60 60**

**Website: www.restaurantlarive.com**

**Description:**

- La Rive is a 2 – Michelin starred restaurant that offers fine dining.
- It has spacious formal dining room with large tables and a great view of the Amstel Dam perfect for people who wants to make a good impression over lunch or dinner
- The menu of the restaurant frequently changes but dishes like turbot and truffle in potato pasta and caviar is a standby.
- Offers great ambience and a scenic view with friendly receptionist.

## *6. OLD SOUTH DISTRICT*

Old South is home to the famous Concertgebouw, various museums, boutiques and chi – chi restaurants! While you're waiting for your seat, you might come across famous violinist Anne Mutter or singer Placido Domingo along the streets of this district. The eastern aside is less formal, and restaurants there offer traditional Dutch dishes as well as tapas. Here are the top restaurants in the Old South district that you can feast on:

**Bark**

**Tel: 675 02 10**

**Website: www.bark.nl**

**Description:**

- This restaurant is just a few distance away from Concertgebouw
- It's a vibrant place that also does pre and post – performance presentations for diners
- Their specialties here include shellfish dishes, smoked oil fish, grilled tuna steak coupled with balsamic sauce and top with bacon.

**Cobra Café - Restaurant**

**Tel: 470 01 11**

**Description:**

- The restaurant's interior and structure is of an artsy glass cube, and it's also filled with original works of Appel, and Corneille that attracts tourists around the area
- This café – restaurant offers one of the best salad dishes in the area; you can also try their special club sandwich or a slice of Karel Appel tart.
- One of the restaurant's unique features is their high – tech toilets that comes with a cost for diners.

## *7. VONDELPARK AREA*

If you just want to relax, eat, and hang out while soaking in the beautiful scenery of Vondelpark, you can try out various restaurants and cafés around the area. Tourists can choose from various coffee shops, and exotic dishes from Asia and Africa. The fresh and earthy vibe of the Vondelpark makes a great dining experience. Here are the top restaurants in the Vondelpark area that you can feast on:

**'T Blauwe Theehuis**

**Tel: 662 02 54**

**Website: www.blauwetheehuis.nl**

**Description:**

- This functionalist teahouse located in a multilevel building that's built in 1936 offers great coffee, tasty cake delights, and different types of alcoholic drinks perfect for tourists who just want to chill and hang out.
- The place also has a terrace and balcony that's great for tourists who wanted to take a sip from their beer and eat a tasty dessert during a sunny day.

**Paloma Blanca**

**Tel: 612 64 85**

**Website: www.palomablanca.nl**

**Description:**

- The name of this restaurant is Spanish but their interiors and equipment ranging from lanterns to mosaic – top tables came from Marrakech souk
- We recommend you trying out their olives and brik (which is a spicy tuna spread) as an appetizer before ordering their main course which is a Moroccan stew dish.
- You can also try their lamb and chicken dishes as well as their grilled spicy sausage

## *8. DE PIJP DISTRICT*

The cuisines and restaurants that you'll find in De Pijp district is filled with various 'flavors.' It has many restaurants that are funky and fashionable that's suited for specific age range. If you want to try unique ethnic places, you can go to the western side of Albert Cuypmarkt. For millennials and up, you can try some restaurants located in the northern area of Marie Heinekenplein Street. Here are the top restaurants in the De Pijp area that you can feast on:

**Puyck**

**Tel: 676 76 77**

**Website: www.puyck.nl**

**Description:**

- This restaurant has a sophisticated cooking approach that's appropriate for a nice dining experience
- Make sure to try their baby lobster dish that's topped with lettuce, or their duck breast that's marinated with the Chinese 5 – spice.
- They also offer a Thai curry flavored ice cream!

**Mamouche**

**Tel: 673 63 61**

**Website: www.restaurantmamouche.nl**

**Description:**

- This restaurant has a great modern – day Moroccan interior that's of a minimalist style; it has mottled walls, slat – beam ceilings, and exposed flooring that complements their overall cuisine and cooking approach.

- They offer various lamb and fish dishes.
- Make sure to get a reservation first

## 9. *PLANTAGE, EASTERN ISLANDS & EASTERN DOCKLANDS*

You can dine in restaurants that are floating above water with a scenic view, and offer an innovative cuisine. Here are the top restaurants in the Plantage/ Eastern Docklands area that you can feast on:

**Plancius**

**Tel: 330 94 69**

**Website: www.restaurantplancius.nl**

**Description:**

- It's just located next to the famous Resistance Museum, and near the Artis Zoo
- Has a very slick and spacious area.
- The place is quite famous because this is where TV executives usually go for their comfort food. They mostly offer pasta dishes.

**Abe Veneto**

**Tel: 639 23 64**

**Description:**

- If you are quite fed up with Dutch cuisine or full – course meals, you can go here and feast yourself with various pizza flavors that use the Dutch stinky cheese.
- They also offer salad, meat, and pasta dishes.

- You can dine out in the terrace especially during summer time.

## *10.OUTER DISTRICTS*

Here are the top restaurants in the Outer District area that you can feast on:

**Blender**

**Tel: 486 98 60**

**Description:**

- The restaurant has a 1970 airport – lounge decoration that attracts youngsters around the area.
- It's a place where you can sip cocktails, groove with the DJ's music spin, and taste a French – Med type of dish

**Betty's**

**Tel: 644 58 96**

**Description:**

- Some locals and tourists consider this restaurant as the top vegetarian place in all of Netherlands!
- The menu they offer each day is just a handful but there's always something new that customers look forward to
- Many people also love their tasty dessert, and decent wine selection

**Café-Restaurant Amsterdam**

**Tel: 682 26 66**

**Website: wwws.cradam.nl**

**Description:**

- It's one of Amsterdam's hippest diners, and it's housed in a former water – processing plant with a 30 meter high wooden ceiling coupled with hanging chains, and metal hooks that adds to its overall ambience.

- They offer a French type of cooking that ranges from mussels, and roasted garlic chicken to star béarnaise.

# Chapter Six: Top 10 Tourist Spots in Amsterdam

To say the least, the city of Amsterdam will sweep any tourists off of their feet! This cozy and connected city is perfect for any type of personalities whether you're an art/history buff, young and adventurous, nature lover, or just a simple tourist looking to escape the trivialities of the modern world as every district within the city has so much to offer.

As with most European cities, Amsterdam is also a place that's bursting with history, culture and the arts. One of the most popular tourist spots that we'll get into later in the chapter includes the poignant Anne Frank House which is the home of Anne Frank herself, who famously wrote her World War II story in her diary, known as Anne Frank's Diary, which eventually became an important piece of literature worldwide. You'll also get to see lots of historical museums, and galleries that housed the works of world – renowned Dutch artists like Van Gogh, and Rembrandt.

If you're not into history, arts, or literature and you're more into the nightlife you can always wander around the famed streets of the Red Light District, the area has an edgy personality to it that also goes beyond stereotypes. You'll find lots of coffee shops, boutiques, waterways, and you can even climb a Dutch windmill, which is what Netherlands is also known for.

If you're still aren't fed up with the charming ambience of the Red Light District, you can always soak in the scenic and picturesque view of the famous Amsterdam canals that's spread out all over the city, through availing canal tours,. The serene and calm vibe that these rivers give off is why most tourists come back, and why some never leave.

In this chapter, we'll take a look at the top 10 most popular and highly recommended tourist destinations in the honest and beautiful city of Amsterdam.

## *1. Museumplein*

This museum is where the 'IAMsterdam' is located. You can take photos of this huge letter slogan with the museum as your background, good luck to having your picture taken though as tourists flock here to get a nice 'Instagram' worthy – shot.

The museum is located in the square, and it's filled with various works of art, and historical artifacts. It's where you can find the famous Van Gogh Museum that houses the largest works of famous and world – renowned Dutch artist, Vincent Van Gogh. You can get to see the different stages of his life through his works of art. This is also where you can find another famous museum called Rijksmuseum; this is where masterpieces of various Dutch artists are housed in, and it also includes lots of historical artifacts. The Rijksmuseum is the oldest museum in the city.

If you're more into the contemporary art, you can visit the Stedelijk Museum as well. Aside from all of these remarkable museum spots, you can also take a walk around the Museumplein where you can find various local shops and fun activities for your family.

## 2. *Anne Frankhuis*

Anne Frank became an international symbol, thanks to her renowned and inspirational diary. In her famous Anne Frank's diary, she told the story of how life was like for her and her family during the time of the Second World War. You'll get to see, experience, and walk through the house where she and her family hid just to escape the vicious wrath of the Nazis. You'll also get to re – read her hopes and dreams through her diary, and learn how the Holocaust and the war impacted the lives of millions from the perspective of a young girl.

It's perhaps one of the best museums not just in the Netherlands but also in the whole world because it's an emotional experience; it's a story that'll get a tug in your heart. It's one of those places where you'll get to really connect with personally because it's alive and filled with love, hope, and inspiration - thanks to Anne Frank.

3. *Amsterdam Museum*

The Amsterdam Museum is best for couples who brought their kids and the whole family. It's a very light and interactive place where everyone can learn a little something about Amsterdam. You can explore everything about the city and how it was built, and how it came about beginning from its ancient roots to the modern – day Amsterdam. You'll get to see artworks, historical videos, graphics, clothing artifacts, and so much more. It's filled with various exhibitions that are perfect for people of all ages. You can also relax and soak in the cultural vibe while having a drink at their Mokum Museum Café located in the courtyard. The Amsterdam Museum is open every day from 10 a.m. until 5 p.m.

## 4. *Amsterdam Flea Markets*

As you traverse the narrow streets of Amsterdam and wander around its outskirts, you'll notice that there are many open – air flea markets. We highly recommend you visiting at least one of them particularly the Albert Cupymarkt which is one of Europe's largest. It offers many organic products, delicious goodies, and it's filled with various stalls where you can buy souvenirs, or cool Dutch memorabilia. You can also try going to other notable flea markets like Noordermarkt and Boerenmarkt which is the hub of book lovers and art buyers as well as the Westermarkt, and Dappermarkt to name a few.

## 5. *Dam Square*

If you want to enjoy the constant hustle and bustle of the city, why not head on over to the Dam Square, where tourists and locals flock; it is a place where you can find various city attractions like the Royal Palace, Madame Tussauds Museum, and Amsterdam's National Monument.

We recommend that you take a tour of the elegant looking and architecturally crafted Royal Palace, take a photo of the National Monument which is a memorial in honor of the victims during the Second World War, and participate in the many events and festivities around the square. It's just a few distance away from the Centraal Station that you shouldn't dare miss.

### *6. Brouwerij t'IJ*

The Brouwerij t'IJ is the best way in Amsterdam to drink beer while admiring the beautiful Dutch scenery. Europeans, particularly the Dutch, Belgians, and Germans are quite known for their great tasting beers. Locals and tourists love going her to have a drink or two while also sightseeing the famous De Gooyer windmill, which is one of the few windmills left in Amsterdam. You can avail tours during the weekends, and go inside the tasting room which opens from 2 p.m. to 10 p.m.

*7. Vondelpark*

If you're a nature lover type, or you simply want to escape the tourist spots and the busy city life, Amsterdam offers many natural spaces for you to relax and feel fresh. Vondelpark is one of the best green parks in the city, and in all of Netherlands. You can take long strolls and bike rides around with your loved ones. You can also bring blankets, foods, and have a picnic on the grass, or better yet read a book while soaking in the lush trees and sunset. We also recommend you to stop by the Blauwe Treehouse which is located in the center of the park. You can go grab a drink while sightseeing the outdoor experience that Vondelpark has to offer. If you come here during the summer, you can also attend an open – air concert for free! Vondelpark is a breather from everything Amsterdam, take the time to visit this place, and just enjoy a moment for yourself.

### 8. *Red Light District*

The Red Light District is locally known as Rosse Buurt, or De Wallen. This area goes as far back as the 14th century.

Back then, it's the hub of sailors if they wanted female companionship. Today, however, it is home to many lit bars, coffee shops, museums, and restaurants, but it managed to maintain its lustful vibe as sex shops, live sex performances, and other erotic activities never went away.

You'll immediately see if you have entered the area because you'll come across short pillars with red lights. If ever you miss such obvious markings, I'm sure you wouldn't miss the clad of women standing in red - lit windows. If you came from a country that has a conservative culture, this place may cause you to have a bit of a culture shock so make sure to research first the places you're going to into. This district is also great for a night out with friends and for couples; it's not suitable for children. If you happen to go here alone, and you're a woman, you might get mistaken for a prostitute, so it's wise that you have someone with you or you're with a group when you visit this edgy and provocative district.

*9. Bloemenmarkt*

If you can't get enough of visiting the open – air flea markets of the city center, why not go to another notable floating market that solely sell flowers? The Bloemenmarkt is the only floating flower market in the world, and it's located on the banks of the Singel Canal near the houseboats. You can buy a piece of the famous Holland Tulip and bring it back home as a souvenir. If you are into the floral world, you can also explore the flower wonderland at Keukenhof but it's only open from March until May. Aside from that, you can also attend a flower auction called Flora Holland which is a one – of – a kind experience.

### *10.Canal Boat Tours*

Perhaps the main tourist attraction of the city is the dams and canals itself. You've never been to Amsterdam if you haven't taken a canal boat tour through these beautiful and scenic rivers. It's best to go early in the morning during sunrise, and in the afternoon during sunset. There's no better way to experience these serene view and the gable houses that abound in the area other than via boat rides.

Amsterdam wouldn't be coined as the "Venice of the North" if it weren't for these canal boat tours. It's the perfect place for couples and families alike. You can pick the kind of boat you'd like to ride, the route you'll take, and the kind of tour you want because some offer a hop – on, hop – off ticket where you can stop by some tourist attractions along the way. Tour prices vary depending on your choice and how many are you in a group. At the time of this writing, the price of the day ticket cost around 22 to 24 Euros. Make sure to do reservations and check prices of the different boat operators in the area. You can also ask if your hotel or accommodation offer canal tours.

# Chapter Seven: Shopping in Amsterdam

Amsterdam was once stuffed with various riches from around the world. It was once one of the centers of trade in Europe. The Dutch empire has come a long way since then, but the good thing is that the people still offered various goods that are quite exotic and rare which you can bring home. You'll find different boutiques and shops that solely devoted to one exotic item/ category like this one store where they only sell nothing but flavored condoms.

Aside from this you can also find other popular items like Gouda cheese, Dutch gin called Jenever, tulip bulbs, old vintage music and designer clothes, rare photographic art, antique shops, custom – made items, and other things that don't even make sense. The best part is that you can get it at a great bargain especially if you purchase from open – air markets.

Amsterdam may not be the haven of high – end boutiques, and it may not be the fashion capital of Europe, but there are a lot of cool and authentic souvenirs that you can only find here. We suggest that if you want to find great and one – of – a – kind items, and cool shops, it is best that you check out the stores along canal houses, and also places like the Negen Straatjes area, Waterlooplein flea market, and cool carts that sell different Dutch items located in the squares. There's something for everyone in the city if you only know where to look. In this chapter, we'll give you the top shopping centers, fashion outlets, and boutiques in every district so that you can have an idea of where to start. Shop 'til you drop!

## 1. *Central Amsterdam*

Central Amsterdam contains the greatest line of stores and multi – level shopping malls. You'll fine various fashion boutiques, high – end and international brands as well as home – grown shops that offers an authentic Dutch style of clothing. You can also wander around the Waterlooplein flea market if you want to grab some cool yet bargain - priced clothes. The city – center also offers amazing and cool items ranging from artworks to books as well as antiques that's great for those who love collectibles. This is perhaps the best place where you can find cool items to take home with you as souvenirs especially for those of you who loves art, books, and collectors. Check out the stores listed below:

**Herman Brood Galerie**

**Tel: 623 37 66**

**Address: Spuistraat 320**

This shop is dedicated to the city's legendary rock singer, and club promoter, Herman Brood. He was once one of the greatest oil painters in the city before his career plummeted due to drug addiction and alcohol. You can purchase some of his great art works or just drop by and appreciate it while you're in the city. The shop can be found upstairs of the bustlin' Café Dante.

**American Book Center**

**Tel: 625 55 37**

**Website: www.abc.nl**

**Address: Spui 12**

The American Book Center is 5 – storey high, and it's one of the biggest English book stores in the city. What locals and even tourists love about it is that its interior design, specifically its floors and décor are very artsy. Any voracious reader will really like hanging out here because of the great ambience. You can  buy a bunch of books that'll piqued your interest, and you can also check out there fiction sections where they have special – interest titles. There's also other genres from non – fiction to periodicals and the likes.

**<u>Athenaeum Bookshop & News Agency</u>**

**Tel: 622 62 48**

**Address: Spui 14-16**

This is another multilevel book store that attracts lots of people wandering around the city – center. You can find lots of usual and unusual book titles as well as international magazines, and newspapers. You'll also be greeted and assisted by their cheerful staff.

## 2. *Red Light District*

The Red Light District is not just home to sex shops or the live nude performances, although this is why lots of tourist comes here. Once you're done wandering around this area, and checking out the 'sinfulness' of this district, you can dine and shop here with your friends and grab some interesting stuff for you to take home. Check out the shops listed below:

**Antiquariaat Kok**

**Tel: 623 11 91**

**Website: www.nvva.nl**

**Address: Oude Hoogstraat 14-18**

This shop specializes in selling a wide range of used antiquarian stock, from coffee – table books to old prints, and other interesting items that will piqued your interest. Old or classic biology books, art – related references and architecture titles are also being sold here.

**Wonderwood**

**Tel: 625 37 38**

**Website: www.wonderwood.nl**

**Address: Rusland 3**

If you want to check out some old Dutch furniture specifically from the '40s and '50s, then head on over to the

Wonderwood. They sell classic Dutch furniture designs that are either originals or replicated. They sell a classic T46 coffee table that's designed by Hein Stolle, Han Pieck, and Gijs Bakker. You can also buy stuff like a box chair that can be folded into a box which you can take with you along with your luggage.

**Geels & Co**

**Tel: 624 06 83**

**Address: Warmoesstraat 67**

If you're into teas and coffee, you can buy stuff here like teapots, and even coffee plungers. Geels and Co. had been operating for 140 years, and it's known as the most aromatic store in the district. They also sell chocolates, and you can check out their mini museum upstairs.

**Hans Appenzeller**

**Tel: 626 82 18**

**Website: www.appenzeller.nl**

**Address: Grimburgwal 1**

This is one of the city's leading designer stores when it comes to gold and stone jewelry. The shop is known for its simple yet strong designs that will surely grab the attention of any passersby. You can also check out other jewelry shops along this road.

## *4, Jordaan*

Boutique stores in the Jordaan district has a home – made and artsy vibe. If you check out the Elandsgracht area, you can find lots of artsy stuff like photography stores, hat shops, and even something for your pet cat. You can also shop in the Haarlemmerdijk area but that's usually where tourists flock. Check out the stores listed below:

**<u>Claire V</u>**

**Tel: 421 90 00**

**Website: www.clairev.nl**

**Address: Prinsengracht 234f**

This store offers handbags made out of silk, embroidered accessories with floral designs and patterns as well as other designer goodies. The clothes being sold here are made by landmine victims in Cambodia, and every clothes you buy will surely help these people out.

**Rock Archive**

**Tel: 423 04 89**

**Website: Www.Rockarchive.Com**

**Address: Prinsengracht 110**

This store offers a limited edition of rock 'n roll prints. It's a professional shop where rock stars like Debbie Harry, Robert Plant, and Sting go to while they're in the city. The store offers clothes that are impeccably designed and slick.

**Josine Bokhoven**

**Tel; 623 65 98**

**Website: www.galeriejosinebokhoven.nl**

**Website: Prinsengracht 154**

This contemporary art store is located just across the famous Anne Frank Museum. You can find lots of artworks created by emerging Dutch artists as well as famous German artist Ralph Fleck.

## *5. Southern Canal Belt*

The Southern Canal Belt is home to sleek Dutch fashion, rare Dutch gins, and antique stores that offer cool collectibles, tribal arts, vibrantly – colored flower shops, and commercials artworks. You can also check out various goodies that are nothing short of staggering. Check out the shops listed below:

**Cityboek**

**Tel: 627 03 49**

**Website: www.cityboek.nl**

**Address: Kerkstraat 211**

There aren't a lot of shops that are selling quality souvenir posters except for Cityboek. It's a small publishing house that sells wonderful, multi – colored and precisely drawn prints, books, and postcards of the city of Amsterdam. If you want to go old school, and share to some of your loved ones back home about this gorgeous city why not buy these beautifully printed postcards, so that you can share with them your experience.

**Decorativa Art & Antiques**

**Tel: 320 10 93**

**Address: Nieuwe Spiegelstraat 9A**

If you're an antique collector, then going to this store will bring you delight as they sell amazing antiques from various European cities. You can also find lots of weird and quite exotic vintage gifts. The interior of the store particularly its ceilings are filled with paintings.

**Eduard Kramer**

**Tel: 623 08 32**

**Address: Nieuwe Spiegelstraat 64**

If you're looking for an authentic home ware antique shop, you can check out Eduard Kramer. They mostly sell antique Dutch floor and wall tiles as well as glass and silver. Your home will surely have that vintage European feel if you buy home wares here.

## *6. Old South*

Shops are concentrated in the Hooftstraat area. This is where you can find many international brands like Chanel, Louis Vuitton, Mont Blanc, Hugo Boss, Dolce & Gabbana, Zegna, and JA Henckels to name a few. You can shop for furniture and secondhand home – design stores at Overtoom which is located just across the Vondelpark. Check out the shops listed below:

**De Winkel Van Nijntje**

**Tel: 671 97 07**

**Address: Beethovenstraat 71**

This is a toy and kids merchandise by popular Dutch illustrator named Dick Bruna. He created a famous Dutch cartoon character known as Miffy, and it's sort of like the "Mickey Mouse" version when it comes to kids' merchandise. You can buy items like pencils, story books, plush toys, soap bubbles, playhouses, and also children's clothing. You and your children will surely enjoy shopping here.

**XSmall**

**Tel: 470 26 00**

**Website: www.xsmall.nl**

**Address: Van Baerlestraat 108**

This is another shop that's targeted for children but aside from toys, they offer cute – as – a – button clothes for kids from aged 0 to 10 years old. They also offer digital photography services where they can take a photo of your little kid and have it framed in an Andy Warhol style.

## *7. Vondelpark Area*

Since this park is quite famous for tourists who love the outdoors, you can find lots of travel and outdoor gear shops in this area. When you're already up for more challenge other than the canal – boat tour, head on over here and shop for equipment that will quench you of your thirst for everything outdoors so you can come prepare for other strenuous activities. Check out the shops listed below:

**Pied À Terre**

**Tel: 627 44 55**

**Address: Overtoom 135**

This is a travel – book shop that's perfect for tourists who will go for outdoor pursuits. You can find travel guides of the city here, topographical maps, and cycling tomes as well as some guide for trekking. The skylit interior has a Renaissance vibe to it making shopping much more interesting.

**Bever Zwerfsport**

**Tel: 689 46 39**

**Address: Stadhouderskade 4**

If you've decided to go out for a hike or even trek and have a Himalayan expedition, you can find everything here at Bever Zwerf Sport. They sell all sorts of camping and mountaineer gears, equipment, shoes, and also durable outdoor clothing.

## *8. De Pijp*

Shoppers usually flock in the Albert Cuypmarkt area of De Pijp, and for good reason. You can find vast number of shops selling almost everything a shopper needs for a reasonable price. Go in this area if you want to buy quality stuff at a bargain price. Even the Queen herself ran out of money when she shopped here to mark the 100th year of the market back in 2005. This is the shop 'til you drop spot in all of Amsterdam. Check out the shops listed below:

**Fietsfabriek**

**Tel: 672 18 34**

**Website: www.fietsfabriek.nl**

**Address: 1e Jacob van Campenstraat 12**

If you fell in love with the biking system of Amsterdam, and you want to go and grab your own set of wheels, then head on over to this wild and crazy workshop where you can buy custom bikes and lots of cool bike designs.

**Stadsboekwinkel**

**Tel: 251 15 10**

**Address: Vijzelstraat 3**

For those of you who are history buffs, this is the shop where you can find the best books regarding Amsterdam's history. You can also buy books that are about the city's urban development, politics, economics, and also environment.

### *9. Plantage, Eastern Islands & Eastern Docklands*

If you happen to own a yacht or a simple boat back home, then this is the best place to shop for a new interior; tourists usually come here for boat equipment and gears as well. Aside from that this area is where you can find custom

– made boxes that are perfect as souvenir gifts. Check out the shops listed below:

**Frank's Smokehouse**

**Tel: 670 07 74**

**Website: www.smokehouse.nl**

**Address: Wittenburger Gracht 303**

Frank's Smokehouse is one of the main suppliers of fish and seafood to the city's major restaurants. They make excellent smoke fish, Alaskan salmon, and they also supply the freshest halibut, and yellowfin tuna which you can buy for yourself. They pack it in using vacuum packs so that it can easily get through airport customs. Check out the fishes here, it'll be worth it!

**De Ode**

**Tel: 419 08 82**

**Address: Levantkade 51**

If you want something morbid to and poignant to bring back home, you can check out De Ode store. This is where you can find bookcases that can be converted to a coffin! They also sell coffin on wheels with a bicycle towbar that's perfect for your 'last bike ride.'

### *10. Nieuwmarkt*

Niewmarkt is located in the city – center. This is where you can find cosmetic items, herbal medicines, and also plenty of artwork shops. Check out the stalls listed below:

**Jacob Hooy & Co**

**Tel: 624 30 41**

**Address: Kloveniersburgwal 12**

This is a cool chemist shop that's been selling medicinal herbs since 1743! When you get inside, you'll see that the interior has huge and old – century walls complete with wooden cabinets and drawers. Aside from herbs, you can also buy various homeopathic remedies, and natural cosmetics as well as medicinal teas.

**Po Chai Tong**

**Tel: 428 49 56**

**Address: Waterlooplein 13**

If you feel stress or tired already from roaming around the busy streets of Amsterdam, you can go to the Po Chai Tong where you'll meet Traditional Chinese Medicine doctor named Dr. Kai Zhang. He sells Chinese herbal medicines, and also offer acupuncture services.

**Typo Gallery**

**Tel: 623 85 52**

**Website: www.ewaldspieker.nl**

**Address: Groenburgwal 63**

This is where you can buy popular artworks made by the artistic and ingenious mind of Ewald Spieker. He creates graphic art out of topography, and his works including books have been exhibited around the world. It'll be an interesting memorabilia to keep and take home.

# Chapter Eight: Museums in Amsterdam

The Van Gogh museum may be something that lots of tourists don't miss during their trip to the city despite of the crowded scene and quite expensive admission, but there are also lots of great galleries and museums that are quite small, independent, and more affordable for the budget traveler. You can spend a day visiting the more prominent museums or galleries but it's also great if you check out other places that features very interesting and unconventional exhibitions. Such places feature contemporary art from young and upcoming Dutch artists while others feature surreal, colorful, and really unconventional type of art like the Condomerie. Whatever it may be, you'll surely enjoy the art and history scene of Amsterdam; you'll also see how their ancestors built the city that it is today, and how forward thinking the new generation is in further shaping the future of the art scene.

### 1. *The Condomerie*

This is one of those galleries or shops that are quite unconventional and very interesting – it's definitely something that the Van Gogh Museum doesn't have. The Condomerie is the first ever specialist condom shop in the whole world! And in Amsterdam, such place is not considered taboo or weird, to them it is art! It's a treasure shop of latex artistry, so to speak. And you guessed it right; it is located in the Red – Light District! It has been displaying colorful and artistic collections of condoms in one of the oldest streets in Amsterdam since 1987!

You can purchase hand – painted novelty condoms that come in different shapes, designs, and sizes. Locals call it the "condom museum," and it was founded by three friends who wanted to break the taboos when it comes to contraception and STDs. It's far more than a museum or a shop, for some, they consider it as an institution that help shape the modern sexual history especially in the city.

**Tel: +31 020 627 4174**

**Website: condomerie.com**

**Schedule: Mon to Sat (11am to 6pm); Sun (1pm to 5pm)**

## 2. *Van Gogh Museum*

The next on the list that everyone goes to when they are in the city is the ever famous Van Gogh Museum. This is where the largest collection of one of the most notable painter of the last century, Vincent Van Gogh, is housed in. You can see and marvel at all his famous works of arts during his lifetime from the Sunflowers, through the Potato Eaters, to the Wheatfield with Crows. You can also see his over 200 other paintings as well as letters, drawings, and artworks that inspired Van Gogh. You'll also see a huge archive of other world – renowned paintings, and prized works from famous artists around the world. We suggest that you make an online reservation before you head here so that you can avoid the long lines.

**Tel: 0031 20 570 5200**

**Website: www.vangoghmuseum.nl**

**Address: Paulus Potterstraat 7, 1071 CX, Museum Quarter**

**Admission: €15 per person; kids that are 17 years old and below are free.**

**Open daily from 9amto 5pm, except Friday until 10pm**

## *3. Stedelijk Museum*

Next to the Van Gogh Museum is the Stedelijk which is also located in the Museum Quarter. The museum has been recently revamped so that it can provide more space to showcase various modern and contemporary arts. Former directors of the Stedelijk Museum way back in the 20th century managed to gather various artworks from the new art movements before the rest of the world noticed them. You can see paintings of artists like De Stijl, Mondrian,

Malevich, CoBra, and Kandinsky. You can also soak yourself with various applied art, video art, and other modern – day murals.

**Tel: 0031 20 573 2911**

**Website: www.stedelijk.nl**

**Address: Museumplein 10, 1071 DJ, Museum Quarter**

**Admission: €15 for adults; students and children aged 13 to 18 cost €7.50 each; children 12 years old and below are free of admission**

**Open daily from 10am to 6pm, except Thursday until 10pm**

### 4. *Hermitage Amsterdam*

The Hermitage Museum was a former almshouse for old people back in the 1680s! Today, it houses various treasures from the Hermitage Palace which is located in St. Petersburg. The artifacts are categorized in various themed exhibitions. You'll surely enjoy marveling at the long refectory that's also complete with century old organs which were used for church services. Tourists are also fascinated with the quite creepy vibe that the Governesses' Room gives off. You can also take a tour at the 18th century cellar kitchen where you can see huge pots that you can climb into to stir it.

**Tel: 0031 20 530 8755**

**Website: www.hermitage.nl**

**Address: Amstel 51, 1018 EJ, Canal Belt**

**Admission: €15 each; children aged 6 to 16 cost €5; children under 6 years old are free of admission.**
**Open daily from 10am to 5pm**

## *5. Droog*

By this point, you may now have learned that the Dutch as a society is artistic, and they take designs very seriously. You can see it in the interiors of their shops, hotels, and suites; from the many artworks that the locals produce over the centuries, and how the founders designed the main city itself, who would've thought that building canals and bridges on every corner makes for a scenic and refreshing view?

When it comes to designs, the Dutch are quite good in thinking out of the box when they're creating materials and designing them out of the ordinary. Such places like Droog. This is a conceptual design studio that's built around the '90s, and remains one of the pioneers when it comes to Dutch design. Tourists and locals alike love visiting the showroom especially those people who are interested in modernist eye candy. You'll see classic works from various designers like Tejo Remy (Chest of Drawers which is made up of assorted wooden drawer), and Marijn van der Poll (stainless steel chair consisting of a metal cube and hammer that you can turn into other shapes) among many.

**Tel: +31 020 523 5059**

**Website: www.droog.com**

**Address: Staalstraat 7b**

**Open from Tues to Sun 11am to 6pm, but closed on Mondays**

## 6. *The EYE Film Museum*

Some of the temporary exhibition at the main EYE film museum requires admission tickets, but if you're on a budget, tourists usually visit the basement because it's free plus you can immerse yourself in everything about cinema. You can also check out their special exhibition rooms like the Panorama room where you are surrounded with 100 movie clips and scenes that are projected on the walls. What many people love about this museum are the so – called viewing pods. Viewing pods are designed and placed in futuristic looking cabins that contain a small couch for visitors to watch the movie.

**Tel: +31 020 589 1400**

**Website: www.eyefilm.nl**

**Address: IJpromenade 1**

**Basement is open daily from 10am to 6pm**

## 7. *City Archive*

The Amsterdam City Archives is a great place to learn more about the city's history through the quirky treasures in its archives. You'll get to see artifacts like a report of a 1942 police that allegedly stole Anne Frank's bike, as well as the telegram about Karl Marx's visit to Amsterdam back in 1872. You'll also get to see photos of music legend, John Lennon as well as Audrey Hepburn. The interior of the City Archives are quite impressive, and you can also see some of the collections are placed within a majestic – looking tiled vault.

**Tel: +31 20 251 1511**

**Website: www. stadsarchief.amsterdam.nl**

**Address: Vijzelstraat 32**

**Open daily except on Mondays; Tuesday to Friday from 10am to 5pm; Sat to Sun noon 'til 5pm.**

## *8. Rijksmuseum*

Another museum that tourists love to flock into is the Rijksmuseum. The museum finally opened its doors at the time of this writing after a decade – long renovation. It houses artworks and other masterpieces like The Night Watch from another famous Dutch artist named Rembrandt. You can also see the works of Frans Hals, Jan Vermeer, Ferdinand Bol, and Jan Steen. Aside from that, you can marvel at the glittery century – old costumes making you feel like you're one of them royals. Tourists also love the $12^{th}$

century Buddhain located in the Asian Pavillion as well as the 17th century – old doll houses.

**Tel: 0031 20 674 7000**

**Website: www.rijksmuseum.nl**

**Address: Museumstraat 1, 1071 XX, Museum Quarter**

**Admission: €15 each; children 18 years old and below are free**

**Open daily from 9 am to 5 pm**

## *9. FOAM Photography Museum*

Photography is the center of focus in the FOAM museum. It doesn't just offer international exhibitions from world – renowned photographers like Richard Avedon and Diane Arbus, it also hold independent and small exhibitions for contemporary photographers in Amsterdam. You can also purchase limited editions of photos with autographs of up and coming photographers as well as signatures from famous names that have graced the museum.

**Tel: 0031 20 551 6500**

**Website: www.foam.org**

**Address: Keizersgracht 609, 1017 DS, Canal Belt**

**Admission: €8.75 each; students and over senior citizens cost €6; children under 12 years old are free**

**Open daily from 10 am to 5 pm**

## *10.Verzetsmuseum (Museum of the Resistance)*

Another fascinating independent museum that history buffs out there would appreciate is the Museum of Resistance. This museum features the life of the Dutch during the time of the Second World War when the Nazis occupied them. You'll also get to see archives such as homemade radios, forged documents, and film footages as well as other materials that tell the whereabouts of the secret underground resistance movement. You'll surely be moved and inspired by all of the stories of these people because it'll give you just a tiny glimpse but a realistic sense of what life was like for them during these dark times.

**Tel: 0031 20 620 2535**

**Website: www.verzetsmuseum.org**

**Address: Plantage Kerklaan 61A, 1018**

**Admission: €8 each; children from 7 to 15 years old cost €4.50; children under 7 years old are free**

**Open daily from Tue to Fri, 10am to 5pm; Sat to Mon, 11am to 5pm**

# Chapter Nine: Nightlife in Amsterdam

The city's entertainment and nightlife scene is quite easy – going, and also diverse for a place of this size. Amsterdam may not be as exquisite compared to other European cities when it comes to the minimalist style interiors of nightlife venues but it still give off that refreshing and relaxing vibe that any tourists will surely enjoy. Dressing up is not a big deal in Amsterdam; you can even go to the theater just wearing a plain shirt and jeans, and people won't mind.

Whether you'd want to spend time watching a play and movies, or partying at nightclubs, the Dutch are pretty casual dressers, so you don't have to worry anything about buying stylish clothing, although they will surely appreciate you for trying. Amsterdam is much like a cosmopolitan village where everyone knows almost everyone!

The city offers various activities that you can do at night by yourself or with a company. You can choose to unwind by going to the movies, watching classical concerts, and visiting performance venues where sometimes opera or ballet activities are being held. The city is also filled with medium to high – end clubs and bars that anyone will surely enjoy; it's also a flourishing art scene where you can visit night galleries if you're still aren't fed up with all the museum tours in the morning. Amsterdam comes alive whenever there are festivities around, and open – air night entertainment along the canals, streets and in parks.

In this chapter, we've listed all the fun and cool things you can do to enjoy the night life in the city. We've also included a list of our suggested places for each activity so that you'll have an idea where to start.

## *1. CLUBBING*

If you and your company like to party or go clubbing, you can do so by going to the city – center area as well as the Southern Canal Belt. This is where all the lit clubs and high – end bars are located. However, if you want to hang out and meet locals, the Dutch usually prefer glitzy and large clubs that are outside of town. Most clubs close at 4 a.m. every Thursday and Sunday, and usually at 5 a.m. every Friday and Saturday. If you're still up for it, you can check out clubwear stores or go to record shops for some after – party experience. Admission in clubs starts at around €20 while other nightclubs are free as long as you purchase some drinks. You might want to give a couple of Euros to the person in charge at the door or the bartender serving you. Here are some of the best nightclubs in Amsterdam that you can check out:

**BITTERZOET**

Tel: 521 30 01

Website: www.bitterzoet.com

Address: Spuistraat 2

**DANSEN BIJ JANSEN**

Tel: 620 17 79

Website: www.dansenbijjansen.nl

Address: Handboogstraat 11

**ESCAPE**

Tel: 622 11 11

Website: www.escape.nl

Address: Rembrandtplein 11

**ODEON**

Tel: 521 85 55

Website: www.odeonamsterdam.nl

Address: Singel 460

**PANAMA**

Tel: 311 86 86

Website: www.panama.nl

Address: Oostelijke, Handelskade 4

**SUGAR FACTORY**

Tel: 626 50 06

Website: www.sugarfactory.nl

Address: Lijnbaansgracht 238

**TO NIGHT**

Tel: 694 74 44

Website: www.hotelarena.nl

Address: Hotel Arena, s - Gravesandestraat 51

**VAKZUID**

Tel: 570 84 00

Website: www.vakzuid.nl

Address: Olympic Stadium 35

**WESTERGASTERRAS**

Tel: 475 14 12

Website: www.westergasterras.nl

Address: Klönneplein 4

**WINSTON KINGDOM**

Tel: 623 13 80

Website: www.winston.nl

Address: Hotel Winston, Warmoesstraat 127

**DE NIEUWE ANITA**

Tel: 415 035 12

Website: www.denieuweanita.nl

Address: Frederik Hendrikstraat 111

**JIMMY WOO**

Tel: 626 31 50

Website: www.jimmywoo.com

Address: Korte Leidsedwarsstraat 18

**POWERZONE**

Tel: 0900 769 37 96

Website: www.thepowerzone.nl

Address: Daniel Goedkoopstraat 1 - 3

## 2. *ROCK, JAZZ & BLUES*

When it comes to attending entertainment and music venues, you can usually just do a walk – in but it's wise to make a reservation ahead especially if famous acts will be performing for that night. We recommend you going to Rock clubs, Jazz clubs, and try to also listen to some Blues music. Jazz is quite popular in the city; you might want to attend the so – called North Sea Jazz Festival which is the largest jazz fest in the city and of the world! In addition to this, you can also hang out in different cafes at night to catch the latest music acts from up – and – coming local artists.

Here are some of the best music clubs and venues in Amsterdam that you can check out:

**BIMHUIS**

Tel: 788 21 50

Website: www.bimhuis.nl

Address: Piet Heinkade 3

**CLUB**

Tel: 623 34 40

Website: www.bourbonstreet.nl

Address: Leidsekruisstraat 6 - 8

**BRASIL MUSIC BAR**

Tel: 626 15 00

Website: www.brasilmusicbar.com

Address: Lange Leidsedwarsstraat 68 - 70

**CASABLANCA**

Tel: 625 56 85

Website: www.casablanca-amsterdam.nl

Address: Zeedijk 26

**COTTON CLUB**

Tel: 626 61 92

Address: Nieuwmarkt 5

**DE HEEREN VAN AEMSTEL**

Tel: 620 21 73

Website: www.deheerenvanaemstel.nl

Address: Thorbeckeplein 5

**JAZZ CAFÉ ALTO**

Tel: 626 32 49

Website: www.jazz-cafe-alto.nl

Address: Korte Leidsedwarsstraat 115

**KORSAKOFF**

Tel: 625 78 54

Website: www.korsakoffamsterdam.nl

Address: Lijnbaansgracht 161

**LISBOA**

Tel: 622 12 72

Address: Veemkade 251

**MALOE MELO**

Tel: 420 45 92

Website: www.maloemelo.com

Address: Lijnbaansgracht 163

**HEINEKEN MUSIC HALL**

Tel: 0900 687 42 42

Website: www.heineken-music-hall.nl

Address: Arena Blvd 590, Bijlmermeer

**PEPSI STAGE**

Tel: 0900 737 74 78

Website: www.pepsistage.nl

Address: Arena Blvd 584, Bijlmermeer

## 3. *WORLD MUSIC*

Central Amsterdam is home to various up – and – coming young Dutch musicians looking to make their mark in the world of music. The kind of sound that they usually play here varies and is inspired from international music. Dance to the beat of the music of Amsterdammers by checking out these places below:

**AKHNATON**

Tel: 624 33 96

Website: www.akhnaton.nl

Address: Nieuwezijds Kolk 25

**DE BADCUYP**

Tel: 675 96 69

Website: www.badcuyp.nl

Address: 1eSweelinckstraat 10

**TROPENINSTITUUT THEATER**

Tel: 568 85 00

Website: www.kit.nl

Address: Tropenmuseum, Linnaeusstraat 2

## 4. *CLASSICAL MUSIC*

Amsterdam's classical music scene boasts many amazing musical acts performed by international and sometimes world – renowned conductors, orchestras, and soloists. Compared to other European cities, classical music and orchestras thrive in this city. They also offer free lunch during concerts particularly at the Concertgebouw, except in summer. Here's where you can catch classical music acts and performances in Amsterdam that you can check out:

**BETHANIËNKLOOSTER**

Tel: 625 00 78

Website: www.bethanienklooster.nl

Address: Barndesteeg 6b

**BEURS VAN BERLAGE**

Tel: 627 04 66

Website: www.beursvanberlage.nl

Address: Damrak 243

**CONCERTGEBOUW**

Tel: 671 83 45

Website: www.concertgebouw.nl

Address: Concertgebouwplein 2 - 6

**CONSERVATORIUM VAN AMSTERDAM**

Tel: 527 75 50

Website: www.cva.ahk.nl

Address: Van Baerlestraat 27

**MUZIEKTHEATER**

Tel: 625 54 55

Website: www.hetmuziektheater.nl

Address: Waterlooplein 22

5. *CINEMA*

If you're a movie buff or a cinephile, you have 45 movie theaters to choose from that's spread out in the city. You can check out the films that will be shown in cinemas or pubs through the Film Ladder listing or online at www.amsterdam.filmladder.nl. AL in Dutch is *Alle Leeftijden* or the movie is suitable for all ages, make sure to check out the movie rating especially if you're going to watch something that's in Dutch with your kids. International screenings usually have Dutch subtitles with them.

One of the best and biggest movie theaters you can go to is called Pathe Cinemas which also have another branch at the De Munt area. Here are the other movie theaters and venues in Amsterdam that you can check out:

**CINECENTER**

Tel: 623 66 15

Address: Lijnbaansgracht 236

**DE UITKIJK**

Tel: 623 74 60

Website: www.uitkijk.nl

Address: Prinsengracht 452

**FILMMUSEUM**

Tel: 589 14 00

Website: www.filmmuseum.nl

Address: Vondelpark 3

**HET KETELHUIS**

Tel: 684 00 90

Website: www.ketelhuis.nl

Address: Westergasfabriek, Haarlemmerweg 8 - 10

**KRITERION**

Tel: 623 17 08

Website: www.kriterion.nl

Address: Roeterstraat 170

**MOVIES**

Tel: 638 60 16

Website: www.themovies.nl

Address: Haarlemmerdijk161

**RIALTO CINEMA**

Tel: 676 87 00

Website: www.rialtofilm.nl

Address: Ceintuurbaan 338

**TUSCHINSKITHEATER**

Tel: 623 15 10, 0900 14 58

Website: www.pathe.nl/tuschinski

Address: Reguliersbreestraat 26-34

## 6. *COMEDY*

The Dutch aren't just fine linguists and has great appreciation for art and style; they also have a keen sense of humor. This is why stand – up comedy thrives in the city. If you want to laugh out loud with local and international stand – up acts, you can visit the 2 premier comedy clubs in in the Leidseplein area. Other comedy clubs offer a variety of acts from stand – up comedy to fast – talking comics, and witty actions. No one is safe from lampooning even the comedians themselves. Here are the best comedy clubs you in Amsterdam that you can check out:

**BOOM CHICAGO**

Tel: 423 01 01

Website: www.boomchicago.nl

Address: Leidseplein Theater, Leidseplein 12

**COMEDY CAFÉ AMSTERDAM**

Tel: 638 39 71

Website: www.comedycafe.nl

Address: Max Euweplein 43 - 45

**DE KLEINE KOMEDIE**

Tel: 624 05 34

Website: www.dekleinekomedie.nl

Address: Amstel 56-58

## 7. *THEATRE, DANCE & SPOKEN WORD*

Amsterdam also has a lively theater scene; if you're up for something like this, you can catch various singing and dancing performances, theater plays, and the gradually becoming popular spoken word acts. However, performances are usually played in Dutch though there are some acts that use the English language especially during the summer season as it is targeted more for tourists. Aside from the list of theater venues below, you can also check out the Koninklijk Theater Carré venue and the

Stadsschouwburg theatre. Here is the best place that you can go to Amsterdam for a night at the theater:

**AMSTERDAMS MARIONETTEN THEATER**

Tel: 620 80 27

Website: www.marionettentheater.nl

Address: Nieuwe Jonkerstraat 8

8. *GAMBLING*

If you have some money to splurge and you want a different kind of fun, then head on over and bet some of your cash at the various casinos in the city. There are plenty of vices that you can try just for fun, or for those of you who are solid gamblers. You can play the common casino games like slot machines, black jack, Carribean stud poker, touch – bet roulette, and other games that involve trying out your luck! Make sure that you bring with you your government – issued ID (showing your date of birth) along with your passport because it is required but keep in mind though, "the House always wins!" Here are some of the places that you can go to Amsterdam for one crazy night! Cheers of luck!

**HOLLAND CASINO**

Tel: 521 11 11

Website: www.hollandcasino.nl

Address: Max Euweplein 62

## 9. *Night Shopping (for Homosexuals)*

If you happen to be one of those shopaholics, you might want to shop around the city at night so that you can also enjoy the scenic view of the river especially the shops that are along the canal belt. Amsterdamers are the type of people that's not lacking in inhibition when it comes to getting what they want and need. You'll soon learn that the shops around the city especially those that are open at night cater to people who may have interesting needs. You'll get to see sex shops here and there, and boutiques that sell interesting and unconventional stuff. One thing's for sure though, you'll leave with less cash, if none at all but you'll get more ideas and a learning experience. Here are some of the shops you might want to check out at night:

**INTERMALE**

Tel: 625 00 09

Website: www.intermale.nl

Address: Spuistraat 251

**VROLIJK**

Tel: 623 51 42

Website: www.vrolijk.nu

Address: Paleisstraat 135

**SHIRT SHOP**

Tel: 423 20 88

Website: www.shirtshopamsterdam.nl

Address: Reguliersdwarsstraat 64

**MR B**

Tel: 422 00 03

Website: www.misterb.com

Address: Warmoesstraat 89

**ROB**

Tel: 625 46 86

Website: www.rob.nl

Address: Warmoesstraat 71

## *10.BARS AND CLUBS FOR HOMOSEXUALS*

As what we've mentioned in the first few chapters, the Netherlands is the first ever country in the world to legalize same – sex marriage back in 2001 which is why it comes as no surprise that the city is one of the world's largest when it comes to the gay/ homosexual scene. Amsterdamers boast that they are the European Gay Capital since they're one of the first to accept gays, lesbians, queers, and transgender.

You can find lots of cool and also friendly party places that are the hub of homosexuals in the city. One of which is called the Warmoesstraat which is located in the Red Light District. They are quite infamous for their fetish bars, darkrooms, and coffe shops. You can also check out pubs in the Rembrandtplein and Leidseplein if you want to sing – along and dance to the beat of various nightclubs and hotel bars around. If you want to have a classy and chill experience with your fellow queers, you can go to the Reguliersdwarsstraat area, although the place comes alive and filled with crowds during the summer because of the huge party being held here.

Here are some of the nightclubs, diners, shops, and activities that you can do if you're one of them homosexuals; Amsterdam welcomes you with open arms:

**CAFÉ BARDEWIJN**

Tel: 420 51 32

Address: Zeedijk 14

**CUCKOO'S NEST**

Tel: 627 17 52

Address: Nieuwezijds Kolk 6

**DE ENGEL VAN AMSTERDAM**

Tel: 427 63 81

Website: www.engelamsterdam.nl

Address: Zeedijk 21

**GETTO**

Tel: 21 51 51

Website: www.getto.nl

Address: Warmoesstraat 51

**MONTMARTRE**

Tel: 620 76 22

Address: Halvemaansteeg 17

**LELLEBEL**

Tel: 427 51 39

Website: www.lellebel.nl

Address: Utrechtsestraat 4

**THERMOS NIGHT SAUNA**

Tel: 623 49 36

Website: www.thermos.nl

Address: Kerkstraat 58 - 60

# Chapter Ten: Off - Beaten Path in Amsterdam

In this chapter, we'll give you a few suggestions of the 'secret spots' in the city that are not the go – to place of tourist crowds, so to speak. When you visit Amsterdam, you'll immediately see crowds everywhere especially in tourist destinations so it'll be a breather if you can get to places that are non – touristy, and a place where you can get a different perspective of the city.

Some of the spots that are listed here are actually 'hidden in plain sight' while some are totally off the grid even for a local.

The off – the – beaten spots that you're about to read are spread throughout Amsterdam while some are quite further from the city – center. You may need half a day to visit some places while others are just around the corner of the bustlin' crowds hiding in plain sight and unknown to most people including the Amsterdamers themselves. However, visiting some places could be harder especially those that are quite far from the city – center because you need to figure out how to get there, when to go, and if the trip is within your budget, but I guess this is where all the fun is! Robert Frost was right; the road less taken by is usually what makes all the difference, and perhaps a journey that you can really call your own.

## *1. In't Aepjen*

The In 't Aepjen is a hidden, cozy, and quiet bar that's smacked right in the middle of the Red Light District. Don't come here if you wish to party or have a loud, crazy experience because it's a pretty quiet place, and people who come here are usually Dutch couples just wanting to have a relaxing time while sipping beers, cocktails or the famous Dutch gin called Jenever. You can also perhaps strike a conversation with the locals dining here or simply enjoy this historical place and its serene ambience.

This bar was built way back during the time where the Red Light District was still the hub of Dutch sailors returning from their long voyages abroad. Back then, sailors come home with monkeys and money. Some of them who don't have enough money to pay for drinks, trade their monkeys just to have booze. Surprisingly, the owner accepted these live monkeys from different parts of the world as payment which is why they ended up having lots of monkeys around the bar, and sometimes sailors who have no place to sleep because they're broke often end up sleeping in the bar with all the monkeys around them. The owner eventually gave the monkeys to the Amsterdam Zoo. Quite the back story isn't it? Keep that in mind while you're sipping your booze quietly, and let the place take you back to those good ol' (monkey – filled) days!

## 2. *De Poezenboot*

The De Poezenboot is the only floating cat boat shelter in the world. This place is located near the Centraal Station and was established in the '60s. If you're a cat lover then this is a must – visit place for you! It's free of admission, although they accept donations to keep the place running. Call up the place or check their schedule online because they're usually just open in the afternoons. Going to this place with your kids is surely a great way to spend your day!

## *3. Wynand Fockink Proeflokaal*

If you're somewhat interested in liquors and perhaps would like to have a free taste straight from the distillery, then head on over to Wynand Fockink Proeflokaal so you can have an amazing learning experience about how the famous Dutch liquors. The place is established in 1679, and they kept the interiors the same way as it was back then. You'll discover how the renowned Dutch drink Jenever is being made, and get to know what a proeflokaal is, which is quite fascinating. Big groups are usually not allowed so it'll probably be ideal that you or your friends split up into small groups. After the tour, you can buy a bottle of your favorite liquor, and even have your name printed in the bottle so that you can have a cool souvenir.

4. *Ons' Lieve Heer op Solder (Our Sweet Lord in the Attic)*

This secret church in the attic is one of the best unknown museums and attractions in the city, and I think it needs to be given a marketing boost because it's quite a fascinating place, although I guess, it's already fine the way it is to preserve its serene ambience, and to be only discovered by people who truly are searching for it. The place also has an interesting back story; it's composed of 3 canal – houses that are secretly connected to one another because this is where Catholic people meet, gather, and worship in secret at the time when Catholics weren't allowed to practice their faith in public.

Beyond this 2 storey church, the interiors and furniture were kept in the same style as it was during the Golden Age, adding to its historical significance. You'll learn something about history, religion, and even architecture when you go here. It's truly a magnificent place that not a lot of tourists and even locals know. Make sure to visit this off – the – beaten place because it's truly a gem of a museum! It may not be as popular as Anne Frank's Museum or the Van Gogh Museum, but it has the same level of historical significance for the city.

*5, Museum van Loon*

Another museum that's quite unknown for many tourists is the Museum Van Loon. Aside from having a gorgeous interior, it has a secret garden that you can go into. It's open to anyone who wants to discover the hidden garden, and the fluffy cat that roams around the area. Some people say that the cat is a spirit animal, but who knows? Only you can discover that for yourself once you come here.

## *6. Begijnhof*

The Begijnhof is becoming a more popular spot for visitors but compared to other famous spots around Amsterdam, it can still be considered off – the – beaten because even if the hofje is quite well – known to tourists, there are still lots of areas that aren't fully discovered. The door in the American Book Center will lead you to the secret Catholic Church where nuns practice their faith, with a group of women who vowed chastity but were allowed to get married. It's quite a fascinating place especially for those who are raised Catholics.

## *7. Van Stapele*

The Van Stapele is one of the best half – secret bakeries in the city, although it's already becoming increasingly popular because of their delicious chocolate cookies. In fact, they are the only bakery in Amsterdam that sells chocolate cookies! You can buy these delightful treats straight out of the oven, and according to locals who always buy here, the chocolate is truly one – of – a kind, and melts in your mouth when you take a bite.

### *8. Kattenkabinet*

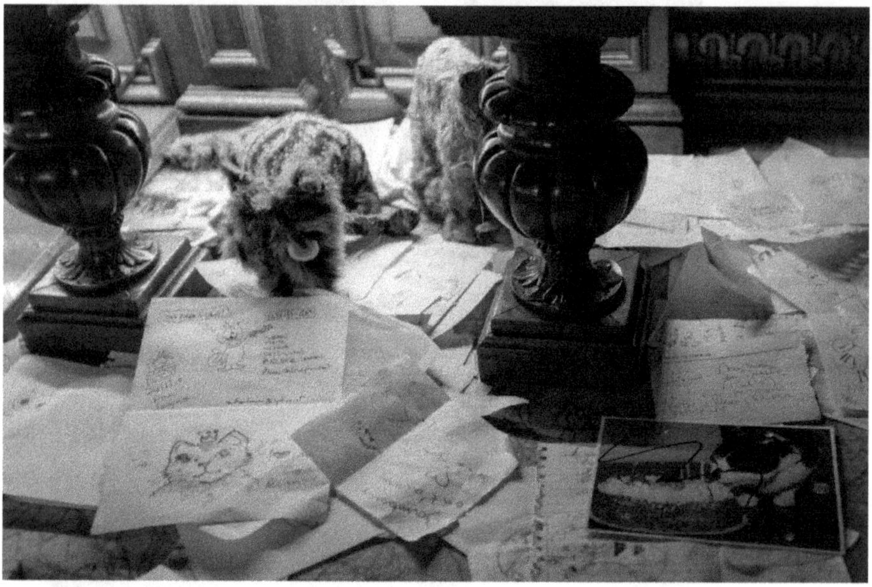

The Kattenkabinet is another off – the – beaten path museum for cat lovers out there! It's a canal house that's not only filled with various cat artworks but also different cat breeds! It's a paradise for cat keepers out there and a cozy place for people who just want to do something different.

## *9. Theatre Tuschinski*

This theater is a must – visit especially if you're a huge fan of movies, but you shouldn't come here just to see a film because the main reason why some tourists come here is for its gorgeous art – deco interior! This movie theater was built in 1921, and it took over 4 million guilders to build this cinema during that time. It's considered a masterpiece then and now. Make sure to also visit the Grote Zaal Theater which is the largest room inside and the architecture and interior is also stunningly beautiful.

## *10.Kinderboerderij 'De Dierencapel'*

The Dutch are quite fond of having green zones or natural areas like spacious parks and trekking locations. If you are bringing your kids with you, the Kinderboerderij 'De Dierencapel' is one of the best playgrounds that you and your children can go to. It's actually more of a children's farm, and you'll soon find yourself playing with cute little bunnies, sheep, and other friendly animals that your children can hang out with.

The best part is that admission is free though they will surely appreciate a donation since the farm is just run by volunteers. The place is also near the canals, and the view around is absolutely gorgeous. You'll surely have a great time in this serene and fun place; you'll also get a chance to talk to some of the locals since not a lot of tourists come here.

# Quick Travel Guide

Amsterdam is a place that has a wealth of history, culture, and beauty. Unlike in other big European cities, Amsterdam has a village – vibe where it seems like everything is within reach, and everyone is your neighbor. I hope you have found the different places in the city to be fascinating, glorious, and also quite weird because that's exactly what the city is about. It's an honest city much like Las Vegas or New York. They have successfully shown the good, the bad, and the ugly but most importantly the collateral beauty. We hope you'll truly enjoy not just the scenic canal river views, or the many historical places that's built here but also the honest and warmth hospitality of the Dutch.

*Amsterdam Quick Facts*

- **Currency** – Euros (€/ EUR)
- **Primary Language Spoken:** Dutch, English, German
- **Weather and seasons:** it has 4 seasons

- **Wet Season**: The rainfalls in the Netherlands are very unpredictable because you can still experience showers even during the dry periods (April to September).

- **Spring and Fall:** March to May and September to October are considered in the country as shoulder seasons. Flowers bloom around May, and the weather is also quite warm around this time which is why it's one of the best times to travel.

- **Summer:** Summers starts from June to August. It's quite hot but not in an extreme way. Summer is the best time to do long walks in the city, and go around it via the canals. Average temperature during summer is around 64 degrees Fahrenheit.

- **Winter:** Winter starts in November until February. You can experience freezing temperatures during these months. Expect a snow and fog in the whole city. The average temperature drops to as low as 2 degrees Celsius. This is why not a lot of tourists go during this period but for some people, they take advantage of the very low hotel/ accommodation rates.

**Best Time to Go**

- Perhaps the best time to go to Amsterdam during summertime is filled with open – air festivities like concerts, theatrical performances, and the likes which are usually free! Tourists and locals also look forward to the Queen's day which is a public holiday that is held every 30th of April

- In addition to all of this, other major cultural events that you might enjoy happens around the month of June (Holland Fest, Roots Music Fest), July (Julidan), and August (Uitmarkt)

- When it comes to accommodation, the best time to go to is around November to December because this is when hotels are very cheap especially around the succeeding months of January to February

## 2. *Transportation*

**Transportation Services in Amsterdam**

**Via Airplane (Schiphol Airport):**

- From the Schiphol Plaza, you can take the Nederlandse Spoorwegen railway to take you to the Central Station. Trains come every 10 to 15 minutes.

Make sure to buy your train ticket before going down to the escalator from the plaza's central court.

**Via Bicycle and Motorcycle:**

- Majority of the locals get around the city using fietsen (Dutch for bikes). There are around 600,000 bicycles around town every day including motorcycles. Tourists usually rent a bike to traverse the city easily.

**Via Canal Boats, Canal Bus, Canal Bikes and Ferries:**

- The Canal Bus Company goes to different routes in between the Rijksmuseum and the Central Station from 9:50 am to 8 pm.
- If you purchase a day pass (€18 for adults; €12 for children), it's valid until noon time of the next day.
- If you want to ride a ferry, you can do so for free! Dock is located behind the Central Station. It may cost you just €1 if the ferry goes to the Eastern Docklands.

**Via Car**

- Foreign tourists are entitled to drive in the Netherlands using their foreign license for only 185 days per year.
- If you're going to stay longer, you must apply for a Dutch license. You can contact the National Transport Authority at 0900 – 07 – 39.
- Local car rental businesses offer a much cheaper rate compared to big companies.
- The rates for local car companies usually start at €34 per day for 2 person cars, and €40 per day for a 4 person car.

**Via Taxi**

- You can hail them at stop zones and at taxi stands which is usually around hotel lobbies. The flat rate is €3.40 and €1.94 per kilometer plus a 5 to 10% tip for the driver.

**Via Train**

- Trains serve the public at regular intervals (every 5 to 6 times per hour) for domestic destinations. The main train station in the city is called the Centraal Station (CS/ Central Station).
- If you are planning to do lot of travelling, then it's best that you purchase a one – day travel ticket which can cost you around €40 at the time of this writing.

## *3. Travel Essentials*

**Money Exchange**

- The currency in Amsterdam and the Netherlands is Euro. 1 Euro is equal to 100 cents.

- You can exchange your national money at various banks and exchanged offices in Amsterdam, or you can also exchange it inside a special office located in the Central Station.

**ATMs and Credit Cards**

- You can withdraw money on various ATMs where major debit cards are accepted.

- There are shops in Amsterdam that doesn't have any cashier, and you can only pay for goods by swiping your credit or debit card so make sure to always bring your card with you, and check if it has a chip on it.

- Credit or debit cards may not come in handy if you're going to eat or buy something from small businesses like food stalls, so make sure to also bring cash with you including coins so that you can easily purchase stuff from vending machines.

**Electric and Voltage**

- The standard electric supply in Amsterdam and the Netherlands is 230 volt to 50Hz AC.

**Communication Services**

- The whole country of Netherlands is serviced by GSM 900/ 1800/ GPRS/ HSPDA mobile networks. If you have a European mobile, you don't have anything to worry about.

- You can use your free Wi – Fi connection at the hotel you're staying in and you can also connect for free when you dine in restaurants, local pubs, coffee shops, and cafes, you may just need to ask the waiters/ staff if it's password protected. You can also go to internet cafes but it will cost you around 2 Euros and it may be quite slow.

## *Amsterdam Highlights*

**Tourist Spots:**

- Museumplein
- Anne Frank's House/ Museum
- Amsterdam Museum

- Amsterdam Flea Markets
- Dam Square
- Brouwerij t'IJ
- Vondelpark
- Red Light District
- Bloemenmarkt
- Canal Boat Tours

**<u>Museums and Galleries</u>**

- The Condomerie
- Van Gogh Museum
- Stedelijk Museum
- Hermitage Amsterdam
- Droog Gallery
- The EYE Film Museum
- The Amsterdam City Archive
- Rijksmuseum
- Foam Photography Museum
- Museum of the Resistance

**Off the Beaten Path**

- In 't Aepjen
- De Poezenboot
- Wynand Fockink Proeflokaal
- Ons' Lieve Heer op Solder
- Museum Van Loon
- Begijnhof
- Van Stapele
- Kattenkabinet
- Theatre Tuschinski
- Kinderboerderij 'De Dierencapel'

# PHOTO REFERENCES

Page 1 Photo by user Anestiev Pixabay.com,

https://pixabay.com/en/street-canal-city-architecture-3279454/

Page 5 Photo by user Medienservice via Pixabay.com,

https://pixabay.com/en/amsterdam-canal-architecture-amstel-3352440/

Page 7 Photo by user Mauro via Flickr.com,

https://www.flickr.com/photos/mauro9/5068228666/

Page 17 Photo by user Christian Grelard via Flickr.com,

https://www.flickr.com/photos/cgre-photos/40385621691/

Page 21 Photo by user Rob Dammers via Flickr.com,

https://www.flickr.com/photos/robdammers/28152104048/

Page 39 Photo by user Diego Portela via Flickr.com,

https://www.flickr.com/photos/diegopf0/18537485986/

Page 53 Photo by user victorsnk via Pixabay.com,

https://pixabay.com/en/street-city-architecture-road-3357547/

Page 55 Photo by user KP Tripathi via Flickr.com,

https://www.flickr.com/photos/kptripathi/6280001086/

Page 59 Photo by user Terretta via Flickr.com,

https://www.flickr.com/photos/terretta/2916127680/

Page 62 Photo by user Valerie Lam via Flickr.com,

https://www.flickr.com/photos/salerie/5959541281/

Page 65 Photo by user Heatkernel via Flickr.com,

https://www.flickr.com/photos/heatkernel/461397350/

Page 68 Photo by user Koocheekoo via Flickr.com,

https://www.flickr.com/photos/koocheekoo/296495309/

Page 72 Photo by user Jorge Franganillo via Flickr.com,

https://www.flickr.com/photos/franganillo/16982606829/

Page 76 Photo by user Sonny Abesamis via Flickr.com,

https://www.flickr.com/photos/enerva/14577197404/

Page 79 Photo by user FaceMePLS via Flickr.com,

https://www.flickr.com/photos/faceme/6426175379/

Page 83 Photo by user Iso Brown FR via Flickr.com,

https://www.flickr.com/photos/isobrown/36518708455/

Page 85 Photo by user FaceMePLS via Flickr.com,

https://www.flickr.com/photos/faceme/5436543052/

Page 89 Photo by user Brando via Flickr.com,

https://www.flickr.com/photos/bpprice/9295232465/

Page 91 Photo by user Jim Forest via Flickr.com,

https://www.flickr.com/photos/jimforest/4433566504/

Page 94 Photo by user Franklin Heijnen via Flickr.com,

https://www.flickr.com/photos/franklinheijnen/15821243556/

Page 97 Photo by user Franklin Heijnen via Flickr.com,

https://www.flickr.com/photos/franklinheijnen/24546619124/

Page 99 Photo by user Garrett Ziegler via Flickr.com,

https://www.flickr.com/photos/garrettziegler/23335282172/

Page 102 Photo by user Garrett Ziegler via Flickr.com,

https://www.flickr.com/photos/garrettziegler/23335234802/

Page 105 Photo by user Stijn Nieuwendijk via Flickr.com,

https://www.flickr.com/photos/stijnnieuwendijk/9672258157
/

Page 108 Photo by user Jan Geerling via Flickr.com,

https://www.flickr.com/photos/microtoerisme/12157676553/

Page 111 Photo by userdeming131 via Flickr.com,

https://www.flickr.com/photos/deming0131/6171475994/

Page 113 Photo by user Steigenberger Hotels via Flickr.com,

https://www.flickr.com/photos/steigenberger/10978744194/

Page 115 Photo by user Franklin Heijnen via Flickr.com,

https://www.flickr.com/photos/franklinheijnen/15477326793/

Page 119 Photo by user Zabara Alexander via Flickr.com,

https://www.flickr.com/photos/zabara_tango/6286147181/

Page 122 Photo by user Elyktra via Flickr.com,

https://www.flickr.com/photos/elyktra/7226548506/

Page 124 Photo by user JPMM via Flickr.com,

https://www.flickr.com/photos/jpmm/25007121189/in/photostream/

Page 125 Photo by user Willem van Valkenburg via Flickr.com,

https://www.flickr.com/photos/wfvanvalkenburg/41863059082/

Page 127 Photo by user Kotomi via Flickr.com,

https://www.flickr.com/photos/kotomi-jewelry/12274513306/

Page 128 Photo by user Kevin Oliver via Flickr.com,

https://www.flickr.com/photos/kmoliver/6913788227/

Page 129 Photo by user Robert Falk via Flickr.com,

https://www.flickr.com/photos/rfalk/4634704495/

Page 130 Photo by user Claudia Regina via Flickr.com,

https://www.flickr.com/photos/claudiaregina_cc/8515503921/

Page 131 Photo by user Not4rthur via Flickr.com,

https://www.flickr.com/photos/pierrotcarre/39686869314/

Page 133 Photo by user Brian Chiu via Flickr.com,

https://www.flickr.com/photos/ecogarden/451012004/

Page 134 Photo by user Anders Sandberg via Flickr.com,

https://www.flickr.com/photos/arenamontanus/7187949812/

Page 136 Photo by user Huub Zeeman via Flickr.com,

https://www.flickr.com/photos/huubzeeman/24654814518/

Page 138 Photo by user Alex DROP via Flickr.com,

https://www.flickr.com/photos/alexdrop/11013689076/

Page 141 Photo by user Teretta via Flickr.com,

https://www.flickr.com/photos/terretta/2915281437/

Page 145 Photo by user Kotomi via Flickr.com,

https://www.flickr.com/photos/kotomi-jewelry/12257188485/

Page 148 Photo by user Timelapsed via Flickr.com,

https://www.flickr.com/photos/timelapsed/16636288134/

Page 151 Photo by user Rodrigo Galindez via Flickr.com,

https://www.flickr.com/photos/rodrigogalindez/3106466032/

Page 153 Photo by user Photo RNW.org via Flickr.com,

https://www.flickr.com/photos/rnw/3118337556/

Page 155 Photo by user Iris Aldeguer via Flickr.com,

https://www.flickr.com/photos/irisux/6674403179/

Page 157 Photo by user Andrei Niemimäki via Flickr.com,

https://www.flickr.com/photos/andrein/3244339291/

Page 159 Photo by user Aaron Butler via Flickr.com,

https://www.flickr.com/photos/pharcyde/2447325308/

Page 163 Photo by user Kotomi via Flickr.com,

https://www.flickr.com/photos/kotomi-jewelry/16309741649/

Page 164 Photo by user Meg Marks via Flickr.com,

https://www.flickr.com/photos/meganmarks/9475222342/

Page 166 Photo by user Salon NYC via Flickr.com,

https://www.flickr.com/photos/isia_tracz/16120335112/

Page 168 Photo by user Sjoerd Los via Flickr.com,

https://www.flickr.com/photos/oxane/5254529706/

Page 170 Photo by user JPMM via Flickr.com,

https://www.flickr.com/photos/jpmm/5036258671/

Page 172 Photo by user derÄsthet via Flickr.com,

https://www.flickr.com/photos/deraesthet/366941663/

Page 174 Photo by user Jim Forest via Flickr.com,

https://www.flickr.com/photos/jimforest/7047831003/

Page 176 Photo by user damian entwistle via Flickr.com,

https://www.flickr.com/photos/damiavos/10538864365/

Page 178 Photo by user erich2448via Flickr.com,

https://www.flickr.com/photos/79369407@N06/8663430664/

Page 180 Photo by user foamamsterdam via Flickr.com,

https://www.flickr.com/photos/foamamsterdam/6321429187/

Page 182 Photo by user damian entwistle via Flickr.com,

https://www.flickr.com/photos/damiavos/10546255845/

Page 185 Photo by user Benito La Malfavia Flickr.com,

https://www.flickr.com/photos/benitolamalfa/14184074601/

Page 187 Photo by user Franklin Heijnen via Flickr.com,

https://www.flickr.com/photos/franklinheijnen/15883640896/

Page 192 Photo by user Marco Raaphorst via Flickr.com,

https://www.flickr.com/photos/raaphorst/420943848/

Page 196 Photo by user André P. Meyer-Vitali via Flickr.com,

https://www.flickr.com/photos/andrepmeyer/4565241339/

Page 198 Photo by user Josh via Flickr.com,

https://www.flickr.com/photos/telemarkskier/5258565215/

Page 200 Photo by user stephanie vacher via Flickr.com,

https://www.flickr.com/photos/trufflepig/137120440/

Page 203 Photo by user Stròlic Furlàn - Davide via Flickr.com,

https://www.flickr.com/photos/strolicfurlan/8637901456/

Page 205 Photo by user Rough Tough, Real Stuff via Flickr.com,

https://www.flickr.com/photos/ensignbeedrill/15055360987/

Page 206 Photo by user Marco Verch via Flickr.com,

https://www.flickr.com/photos/30478819@N08/6257188232/

Page 208 Photo by user ashton via Flickr.com,

https://www.flickr.com/photos/8364994@N02/4834812743/

Page 210 Photo by user tour geek via Flickr.com,

https://www.flickr.com/photos/tourgeek/15209498834/

Page 214 Photo by user Rob Dammers via Flickr.com,

https://www.flickr.com/photos/robdammers/16967578608/

Page 216 Photo by user Seth M via Flickr.com,

https://www.flickr.com/photos/thalamus/15398275529/

Page 218 Photo by user Antony Stanley via Flickr.com,

https://www.flickr.com/photos/antonystanley/302113925/

Page 219 Photo by user vgm8383 via Flickr.com,

https://www.flickr.com/photos/vgm8383/3719888023/

Page 220 Photo by user Tine van Voorst via Flickr.com,

https://www.flickr.com/photos/tinamonumentalia/143363465
29/

Page 222 Photo by user Kotomi via Flickr.com,

https://www.flickr.com/photos/kotomi-jewelry/8445186301/

Page 223 Photo by user Bert Kaufmann via Flickr.com,

https://www.flickr.com/photos/22746515@N02/4151159388/

Page 224 Photo by user albedo20 via Flickr.com,

https://www.flickr.com/photos/albedo20/21646112001/

Page 225 Photo by user Michael Cisneros via Flickr.com,

https://www.flickr.com/photos/125093064@N07/17393873818
/

Page 226 Photo by user G Travels via Flickr.com,

https://www.flickr.com/photos/g_travels/2564567551/

Page 227 Photo by user Merlijn Hoek via Flickr.com,

https://www.flickr.com/photos/merlijnhoek/14354679215/

Page 280 Photo by user Bonnie Carroll via Flickr.com,

https://www.flickr.com/photos/bonniecarroll/8093606784/

# REFERENCES

"Amsterdam" – Wikitravel.org

https://wikitravel.org/wiki/en/index.php?title=Amsterdam&mobileaction=toggle_view_mobile

"A Brief History of Amsterdam, Netherlands" – LocalHistories.org

http://www.localhistories.org/amsterdam.html

"A Look at Dutch Language, Culture, Customs and Etiquette" – Commisceo - Global.com

https://www.commisceo-global.com/resources/country-guides/netherlands-guide

"Do's and Don'ts in Amsterdam" - TravelDudes.org

https://www.traveldudes.org/travel-tips/dos-and-donts-amsterdam/26981

"When to Go in Amsterdam" – Frommers.com

https://www.frommers.com/destinations/amsterdam/planning-a-trip/when-to-go

"Getting Around In Amsterdam" - AwesomeAmsterdam.com

https://awesomeamsterdam.com/getting-around-in-amsterdam/

"Amsterdam Guide" – Tripomatic.com

http://guides.tripomatic.com/download/tripomatic-free-city-guide-amsterdam.pdf

"Introducing Amsterdam" – MIT.edu

http://web.mit.edu/zoz/Public/lp/lp-amsterdam.pdf

"10 Best Attractions to Discover the Essence of Amsterdam" – 10Best.com

https://www.10best.com/destinations/netherlands/amsterdam/attractions/best-attractions-activities/

"20 Essential Things to do in Amsterdam" – Timeout.com

https://www.timeout.com/amsterdam/en/things-to-do/20-essential-things-to-do-in-amsterdam

"10 Top Tourist Attractions in Amsterdam" – 10Best.com

https://www.10best.com/destinations/netherlands/amsterdam/attractions/best-attractions-activities/

"Top 10 Things to Do in Amsterdam" - TripSavvy.com

https://www.tripsavvy.com/best-things-to-do-in-amsterdam-1456851

"Amsterdam's best museums and art galleries" - Telegraph.co.uk

https://www.telegraph.co.uk/travel/destinations/europe/netherlands/amsterdam/articles/Amsterdams-best-museums-and-art-galleries/

"Undiscovered Amsterdam: Off The Beaten Path" – NomanBefore.com

http://nomanbefore.com/amsterdam-discovered/

"Off The Beaten Track: Amsterdam Noord" – YourWatchDutchGuide.com

https://www.yourdutchguide.com/off-the-beaten-track-amsterdam-noord/

www.ingramcontent.com/pod-product-compliance
Lightning Source LLC
Chambersburg PA
CBHW071412090426
42737CB00011B/1434